IN THE LINE OF DUTY:
The Service and Sacrifice of America's Finest

by Constance Clark

with a Foreword by

Craig W. Floyd, Chairman
The National Law Enforcement Officers
Memorial Fund

POTOMAC PUBLISHING
1989

Cover photo courtesy of
Weinbrenner Shoe Company, Inc.

ACKNOWLEDGEMENTS

I wish to thank all the survivors who so generously shared their stories for this book. Thanks to every one of you for granting me the privilege of writing about the loved ones you have lost and the lives you are now leading.

I am grateful as well to Officer Dewey Stokes, National President, Fraternal Order of Police, and to James W. Scutt, Director, Legislative Affairs, National Sheriffs' Association, who provided much valuable insight into the life of a law enforcement officer. And, for their extraordinary inspiration and assistance, I thank Special Agent James Horn of the FBI Academy's Behavioral Science Services Unit, and Detective Richard Pastorella, New York Police Department, founder of the Police Self-Support Group.

Thanks are due as well to Kelley Lang of the National Law Enforcement Officers Memorial Fund, Linda Allison of Potomac Publishing, and Sharon Barnes for their indispensable research and editorial assistance.

Last but far from least, this book could not have been created without the vision and guidance of Craig W. Floyd of the National Law Enforcement Officers Memorial Fund and Robert Allen of Potomac Publishing.

—*Constance Clark*
September 1989
Alexandria, Virginia

ACKNOWLEDGMENTS

DEDICATION

This book is dedicated to all the officers who have risked or lost their lives for the protection of others. Because you care, we care.

FOREWORD

On May 15, 1989, a crowd gathered on the grounds of the United States Capitol. They had been invited by the Fraternal Order of Police Ladies Auxiliary (FOPLA) for the 8th Annual Peace Officers Memorial Day Service.

Bagpipers played and people spoke. President George Bush came and gave a speech about drugs and crime in America. As he left, a choir sang. A steady spring rain drizzled down, soaking the thousands of people who had come to pay tribute.

Then the ceremony really began.

One by one, the names were called out, by FOPLA President Suzie Sawyer, names of law enforcement officers who died in the line of duty in 1988. And as each name was read, a widow, or a mother, or a child, or a whole family would step forward and place a flower in a gigantic wreath.

Some were stoic, as if they had learned to manage their pain, at least in public.

Some wept. Some needed assistance in returning to their seats.

Around them, the colleagues of their loved one stood proudly in uniform for two hours, impervious to the soaking rain.

Mourners placed 161 flowers in the wreath, each representing a death that had taken place the year before—the loss of a man or woman who willingly undertook risks most of us would never even consider taking.

As members of "the thin blue line," they risked their

lives every day to protect their communities and their nation from the terror and destruction of crime.

They were always there when we called, always ready to help, whatever the personal cost to them might have been.

Yet our nation seems to have simply forgotten their service—their sacrifice.

Though an estimated 30,000 law enforcement officers have died in the line of duty since America's beginnings, we as a nation have created no monument to honor their sacrifices. There's no stately building or peaceful garden dedicated to their memory. There's not even a plaque!

Of course, these fallen heroes are remembered by their families and friends. But, as years pass, the newspaper clippings yellow and crumble. The flowers so carefully saved from the funeral spray turn to dust. The children grow up and wonder, "Why did Dad give his life? And why doesn't anybody else care that he's gone?"

As Chairman of the National Law Enforcement Officers Memorial Fund, I believe that people do care – but that many of us, busy with our own preoccupations, overlook the need to pay homage to those who give their lives in our service.

I believe most Americans are not even aware that a law enforcement officer dies in the line of duty *every 57 hours* in our country—an average of 153 each year.

It is my hope that once people learn about the sacrifices that are made on their behalf, they will want to join together to say "thank you" to our law officers, the veterans of America's war on crime, just as they have honored our military heroes. That is why I hope to distribute this book to thousands of Americans who simply aren't aware of the debt we owe to the men and women of law enforcement.

The officers' sacrifices have been too long overlooked. Surely, these men and women deserve nothing less than our respect, our gratitude, our praise, expressed prominently and permanently in our nation's capital!

After two hundred years of silence, the United States of America has at last decided to say "thank you."

In 1984, Congress approved the concept for a National Law Enforcement Officers Memorial. They said we could build our Memorial in Judiciary Square, in the heart of Washington, D.C.

But they also mandated that all the funds needed to build and maintain the Memorial—an estimated $5 million—would have to be raised from the public. Not one cent of government money could be used. Congress also mandated that the money be raised, and ground broken for the Memorial's construction, within five years.

To date, the Memorial Fund has received thousands of contributions, from law enforcement groups and from Americans in all walks of life, Americans who believe in law and order, who support the efforts of our Federal, State, and local officers. But the need is still great.

In creating the concept for this book, I wanted to make sure I could hand it to a stranger and say, "Here. Read this. Then you'll understand why we need to build a National Law Enforcement Officers Memorial—*now.*" Here are stories of the officers who risked their lives and lost them. Here, too, are the stories of those who were permanently disabled in a line-of-duty incident.

And here are the stories of the families, the survivors—those who so courageously face a future without their husbands, wives, fathers, mothers, children, sisters, or brothers.

Mrs. Connie Miller, whose daughter, Hillsborough County (Florida) Sheriff's Deputy Donna Miller, died in a line-of-duty accident, explained the need for the Memorial simply and perfectly: "That Memorial is so important, because when it's built, we can go up there. We can talk about it, and we can cry. We'll know that everybody's there for the same reason we are. And we'll know that Donna has not been forgotten."

With the help of people like you, the Memorial will be built. It will be a place for remembering, a place for healing. It will honor the dead, comfort the survivors, and tell the officers still on the streets that we as a nation care about the dangerous and difficult work they do to protect us, to preserve our very way of life.

As you read this book, please ask yourself one question: Do these officers deserve a permanent, national tribute? Is it our duty to make sure that they will never be forgotten?

If your answer is "Yes," please do your part to help build this long-overdue Memorial. Say your personal "thank you" to the officers who make it possible for you to walk down the street in safety.

Their families—and the entire law enforcement family—will appreciate it.

—Craig W. Floyd, Chairman
National Law Enforcement
Officers Memorial Fund

New Jersey State Trooper Phil Lamonaco

It was just before Christmas—December 21.

New Jersey State Trooper Phil Lamonaco was on his last late duty shift before Christmas. Patrolling a stretch of highway, he pulled a car over for a routine traffic stop.

As he walked in the snow from his cruiser to the car, perhaps Phil was thinking about his wife and children waiting for him at home, getting ready to celebrate a wonderful Christmas. Maybe he thought to himself, "Just a few more hours, and I'll get to go home, look in on the kids, talk with Donna, put a few final touches on the Christmas tree."

Phil Lamonaco never made it home.

Unknowingly, he had pulled over a car carrying two hardened criminals—two men named Manning and Williams, part of a self-proclaimed revolutionary gang called the United Freedom Front. These terrorists were plotting to overthrow the United States government.

Phil saw that Manning had a gun. He asked him to get out of the car. Phil took the gun and started to frisk Manning.

To break Phil's concentration, Manning started waving his arms. As if on signal, Williams jumped out of the passenger side of the car and started shooting.

Williams pumped nine bullets into Phil Lamonaco. The fatal bullet pierced his heart.

It's some consolation to Donna to know that Phil died instantly. But it doesn't help much when she thinks of her husband lying face down in the snow, bleeding.

Manning and Williams were about to speed off into the darkness when Manning decided to retrieve his gun from Phil's body. For a parting shot of incredible viciousness, he then shot Phil three more times in the back of the head.

As her husband was being murdered, Donna Lamonaco was making Christmas cookies with the couple's three children, Laura, 5, Michael, 4, and 10-month-old Sarah. Each of the children had made one special cookie for Daddy to enjoy when he got home.

"We were cleaning up. I was washing flour and sugar off of Sarah around five o'clock when the doorbell rang. Laura had just finished her own bath. She yelled, 'Mommy, there are two men at the door, and I'm stark naked!'"

Laughing, Donna told Laura to get dressed. With little Sarah in her arms, she went to open the door. There she saw two State Troopers, close friends of Phil's and Donna's.

"I thought they had stopped by for a cup of coffee," Donna says. But one of the Troopers, who had a baby close in age to Sarah, took her out of Donna's arms.

They told Donna to sit down. "Phil's been hit," they said.

"It didn't sink in at first," Donna says. "I thought, 'By a car or truck?'"

"No, babe, Phil's been shot," one of the Troopers told her. It was hard to believe that somebody like Phil—so careful, so good at his job, Trooper of the Year in 1979—could get into serious trouble. Donna recalls, "I knew that he would be okay, though, since he had his vest on." Phil and Donna had made a special pact that he would always wear his bullet-resistant vest.

Donna found a babysitter and went with the Troopers to the hospital. "I knew he'd be all right. But when I got to the hospital, they told me: 'Donna, he's gone.'"

It took a while for Donna to comprehend that Phil was actually dead. She wanted to see him for herself: "If I could just *see* him, *hold* him in my arms, I could prove they were wrong—that Phil was okay."

Donna ran down the hallway. "When I saw all the police officers standing outside the door of one room, I knew this was where he was. As I entered the room, cold and still, I felt fear. I wanted to hold him, touch his hand, but because of the many wounds, I couldn't."

Instead of reassuring herself as she had hoped to do,

Donna now had to find a way to tell her children that their Daddy was dead.

The family's pastor brought Donna home from the hospital and tried to explain to the children what had happened. He avoided certain stark words, certain harsh realities. The children didn't understand. Finally, Donna interrupted when Laura asked a question.

"Laura, Daddy died."

In a voice Donna will never forget, her little daughter said, "He _died?_"

Together, Donna and her children buried Phil on Christmas Eve.

It was the worst Christmas of their lives. But, though Phil died in 1981, Christmas is _still_ hard for the Lamonacos.

"Holidays are still the pits for us," she says. "Two years ago, Christmas was really emotionally difficult because the trial was going on, and all the horrifying details that came out made the anger, fear, and loneliness even stronger. And last year was really bad, too. I couldn't figure out why—I didn't even try to. Then in January it hit me. This past Christmas marked the time when Phil had been gone longer than we had been married."

A deeply caring man, Phil was a wonderful husband and father. He and Donna were deeply in love. "Some of the guys would go out for a drink after their shifts, and they'd ask Phil to come along. He'd say no, and they'd tease him about being tied to my apron strings. But he'd say that wasn't it. 'I just love my wife,' he'd say. And he'd come home."

Together, Phil and Donna were building a strong

foundation for their family. They especially loved Christmas, a time of sleigh rides in the snow, hot cinnamon-scented apple cider by the Christmas tree, a tradition of opening one gift each on Christmas Eve.

And every year as Christmas approached, Donna and Phil set up a manger in the living room. They explained to the kids that each time they did a little chore around the house—like putting away their toys—they were entitled to take one piece of straw and put it in the manger, to make a soft bed. They'd start on December 1, and by the time Christmas Day arrived, the manger was ready, a birthday gift for Jesus.

"We had a Currier & Ives, Vermont-style Christmas. There was so much warmth and love." Since Phil's death, it's just routine. On December 21 each year, Donna does something with the children in the morning, then she has her quiet time. "That's my day," she says. "I have to have it." On Christmas Day, they go through the motions, opening presents and joining the family for a holiday dinner.

But Christmas will always be painful for them—Christmas Eve an ever-recurring reminder of the day they buried Phil.

Donna Lamonaco says it's been a real· struggle to pick up the pieces and go forward. Her involvement with other survivors and the National Law Enforcement Officers Memorial Fund has been a big help.

"My children have grown in strength each day. I have shared my involvement with COPS [Concerns of Police Survivors], the Memorial, and law enforcement with my children. They've been a part of this. They are learning to focus their emotions and energies in a positive way." Proudly, Donna tells the story of how her kids comforted other bereaved children.

"An officer was killed, and it happened that he and his family lived next door to a close friend of mine. My friend called me and told me what had happened. I took the kids and we went over there.

"The widow was at my friend's house with her two little ones. She hadn't told her kids yet. She went into the next room to tell them. We heard them crying. It was heart-breaking.

"The door opened, and the little boy looked at Michael. He said, 'Can I talk to him?' My children went in to the other children. Laura put the little girl on her lap, and Sarah stroked her hair. I heard Michael saying to the little boy, 'You know what, little guy? You're gonna be okay. Look at me. My dad was a police officer too. I was the same age you are now when he died. And now I'm 11. You just stick by your Mom and it will be okay.'"

Donna and Phil's youngest, Sarah, spoke words of comfort, too.

"I didn't even know my Daddy, but I know he's someone I'll never forget."

A few days later, Donna returned for the officer's funeral, bearing gifts from her children to the officer's son and daughter—a teddy bear wearing a badge for the boy, and a special doll for the girl. The children just seem to know you need something in your arms at a time like this.

"I was so proud of my children!" Donna says. "It was a reflection of all the work I've done, all the events they've been a part of, from memorial services to television and radio appearances."

Like many police survivors, Donna has tried to make the best of her life in the wake of incalculable loss. "The trial is still going on, and that's hard," she says. "Manning was convicted, but for some reason, the jury came back hung on Williams, so there will be a retrial next year." In the courtroom, Donna suffered the difficulties faced by many survivors—the mandate that she not show emotion, the pain of re-living her husband's death in painful detail. But she also encountered some special indignities.

"Manning and Williams had their comrades in the courtroom with them. None of them would rise when the judge came in, because they didn't believe in the justice system. But when Manning and Williams came in the room, they stood up and raised their fists and shouted a special chant that meant 'victory.'"Because the defendants were well-known terrorists, convicted previously of bombings and armed robberies, everyone entering the courtroom had to be searched. One day, a reporter complained to defense attorney William Kunstler (a former member of the radical Chicago Seven) that Donna was not being searched as thoroughly as some others were. Kunstler insisted that Donna be searched again.

"The justice system is just incredible," Donna said. "The judge told the jury that they must ignore the fact that these men were convicted bombers, thieves, and terrorists determined to overthrow the United States!"

Donna sees little fairness in the system. "Take Manning," she says. "He's in prison. He's lifting weights and he pulls a muscle. They drive him to the hospital, they examine him, they give him liniments and painkillers, and they drive him back. And we're all paying for it."

By contrast, the Lamonacos' health insurance was cancelled immediately after Phil's death. Donna had to search for new insurance. There are many expenses her policy doesn't pay for.

"I go to the doctor with a kidney problem and he prescribes medication. I go to the drug store, and it costs $89, right out of my pocket. It just doesn't make sense that Manning gets his medical care free, courtesy of people like me, when he helped kill my husband!"

Donna has found meaning in her life by helping other survivors through the COPS organization and by helping the Memorial Fund.

"I'm glad to tell my story, because it's a way of doing something good. The more I get involved with lectures, with law enforcement agency work, with widows, the more good I'm doing. I could never give this work up. It's way too important to me.

"Phil chose to be a Trooper," Donna continues. "I choose to walk the path of law enforcement as well. I hope to encourage the police officers who are working our streets. I want to help them walk that path of pride, integrity, loyalty, and honor."

For Phil's sake and for their children's sake, Donna wants to see the National Law Enforcement Officers Memorial built. "The Memorial means so much to me personally, professionally. My efforts, the hard holidays, the loneliness that doesn't go away—the Memorial gives meaning to all of it. All the tears I've shed, all the smiles I show, all my tiredness—part of it all goes to that Memorial.

"When it's finished, we'll be able to stand in front of that Memorial and say 'It was all worth it.' The Memorial will tell all our officers that we honor, respect, and love every one of them. My kids will be able to be so proud of their father, because he chose to help society, and now he'll never be forgotten.

"And on the days when our children wonder why their Daddy ever got involved with law enforcement work and gave his life up serving others, they can think of that Memorial and know that the nation has said 'We will never forget.'"

Detective Michael Raburn
King County (Washington) Police Department

◆◆◆

IT'S ONE OF THE HARDEST JOBS
IN THE WORLD

WANTED: Strong, intelligent, caring, dedicated men and women for public service position. Motivated by a desire to help others. Willing to put your life on line every day. Must tolerate mountains of red tape and bureaucracy, yet be decisive, courageous, and quick on your feet. Salary: Substantially less than what you might earn elsewhere. Recognition: Little to none.

Studies rank being a police officer high among the most stressful, dangerous jobs you can get. That's no surprise to anyone who's ever tried it.

Unlike some hazardous jobs, it doesn't pay very well. In a major city like New York, a senior officer with 20 years of distinguished service might earn $40,000—not a lot when you consider the area's high cost of living. But elsewhere in the United States, that salary would seem like a fortune to police officers. In 1988, the Fraternal Order of Police had legislation introduced in the Alabama State Legislature requiring that rookie police officers earn a minimum of $10,000—little more than minimum wage.

The law hasn't passed yet.

Like many other jurisdictions, the Alabama legislature says the state doesn't have the funds to pay more. Often, law enforcement officers across the nation must work part-time jobs starting after their regular shifts, usually as security personnel for stores and office buildings or special duty assignments.

"We shouldn't pay our law enforcement officers so little that they have to go work a four- to six-hour security detail to make ends meet," says Jim Scutt, a former Alexandria, Virginia police officer now serving as Director of Legislative Affairs for the National Sheriffs' Association. "That means the officer's getting six hours of sleep at night. Citizens are getting short-changed. And when officers get tired, they get careless, and that means they get killed."

Compensation is not the only area where police are getting less than a fair shake. Many don't even have the equipment they need. Police departments have been forced to hold bake sales and raffles to raise money to buy bullet-resistant vests, life-saving equipment that should be standard issue for all law enforcement officers. Some departments still don't have them.

The importance of having the right equipment increases with the escalating violence of America's drug wars. Forced to send officers out into the streets armed with standard service revolvers, chiefs of police acknowledge their men and women are out-gunned by drug dealers carrying expensive semi-automatic weapons.

Soon after the stabbing death of her husband, Detective Michael Raburn of the King County, Washington Police Department, Linda Raburn told a reporter from *The Seattle Times* that Michael's death might have been prevented, were it not for budget cuts.

Linda, a radio dispatcher for the King County Police, remembers that in the early 70s she routinely punched names into the Sea-King (Seattle-King County) crime-computer system. Sometimes a name would come up with the words "HAZARD, HAZ-

ARD" flashing at the top of the screen. Dispatchers could then warn officers that they were dealing with a person who had a history of criminal behavior—particularly assaults upon police officers.

The system provided officers with a major advantage: foreknowledge of a suspect's potential violence. In spite of its enormous value, however, the Sea-King crime computer was all but eliminated because of governmental cutbacks, and Michael Raburn was not alerted to the fact that the man he was to serve an eviction notice on, Robert Baldwin, had threatened police with a rifle the year before.

On March 27, 1984, as Detective Raburn tried to talk to Baldwin through a crack in the apartment door, Baldwin drove a three-foot-long gold, ceremonial sword into the officer's chest. Raburn, a 12-year veteran of the force, died an hour later.

"I keep thinking that if we still had Sea-King, Michael would be alive. Where do you cut a budget when somebody's life is at stake?" Linda Raburn asked.

"A simple eviction notice, a procedure Mike had probably done hundreds of times—that eviction notice and the events that followed would take our Michael away from us forever, crushing all our dreams in the seconds it took for Robert Baldwin's sword to find its mark in Michael's heart," Linda wrote. His loss was especially difficult to accept because of the possibility that it might have been prevented—had the police department had adequate financial support from the community.

The value of other, seemingly less vital equipment can also be underestimated. Most officers in America drive non-air-conditioned cruisers, regardless of the climate. On a hot, humid day, the last thing an officer wants to do is put on another piece of clothing—like a bullet-resistant vest. To encourage all officers to wear vests at all times, says Dewey Stokes, National President of the Fraternal Order of Police, they must be provided with lighter vests and air-conditioned cars.

Low pay and inadequate equipment are just part of what our law enforcement officers deal with daily. The danger and the stress of the job pose the greatest challenges. Every day, police officers come face to face with human misery—a side of life the rest of us encounter only rarely.

Detective Richard Pastorella, founder of the Police Self-Support Group, has been there. In his 23 years on the street with New York City Police Department, he saw it all.

"I can't begin to tell you the effect it has when you see a child that's been killed, an older person that's been mugged," he says. "You see people's problems day in and day out. You build up a wall, because you have to."

For police officers, each accident, each felony, each apprehension is an injury to the human spirit, an injury that rarely has a chance to heal before the next incident demands their full attention.

The stress is compounded by the frustrations of our judicial system and overcrowded jails, by the growing efficiency of professional criminals, and by what many officers perceive as a negative attitude toward them on the part of the public.

Law enforcement officers hear few, if any, words of thanks.

"Very seldom does a citizen come up to a police officer and say, 'Thank you, you did a great job,'" says Pastorella. "You get the tributes when you're dead—but it's too late then. Who do the accolades go to? They go to the family. What good does that do?"

Instead of gratitude, the public often responds with hostility to police officers. One police widow says, "Let's face it, everybody hates the guy who gave him the speeding ticket." But few people realize that more Americans are killed on our highways each year than die from murder or drugs. Police patrolling the highways are just trying to save lives.

Reports and rumors of police brutality—often exaggerated—have added to the problems officers face. In response to community pressure, departments must suspend officers involved in shootings and other, less serious incidents, making them feel as if *they* are at fault when, in fact, most of them were just doing their jobs.

So what kind of a person wants this kind of job? Given the low pay, lousy hours, physical danger, emotional stress, and lack of appreciation, what kind of man or woman actively seeks out a career in law enforcement?

For the most part, it's people who care about people—who feel a real need to serve others. The individuals profiled in this book are typical members of the law enforcement community. They're people for whom service to their fellow human beings outweighs the danger, stress, and other problems of police work—people like Officer John Utlak of the Niles, Ohio Police Department.

Officer John A. Utlak
Niles, Ohio Police Department

◆◆◆

"I'M JOHN, YOUR FRIEND, AND I'M A POLICE OFFICER."

"Did he call for me? Did he holler 'Mother, Father'? If he had been found sooner, could he have been saved?"

Seven years after her son's death, Irene Sudano is a grieving mother. Though doctors have told her that nothing could have saved him once the bullets were fired, her thoughts return again and again to her son, sprawled in the snow, dying alone.

She wishes she could have done something—anything—to keep Johnny alive, or at least to hold him in her arms as he died. But the two young men who killed Officer Utlak didn't give her that opportunity.

John Utlak always wanted to be a policeman. "Even when he was a little thing, he would watch the police shows, like 'Dragnet,' says his mother, Irene Sudano. "He always knew who did it. And when he was a teenager, he'd practice being a detective.

"He followed his dad around town for two days once, and Joe never knew it!"

Motivated by his desire for a career in law enforcement, Johnny was a honor student in high school. He went on to major in criminal justice at Youngstown State University, where he was a member of the Army ROTC. As a sophomore, he was unanimously elected Cadet of the Year. It was the first time this honor had ever been awarded to an underclassman.

Irene Sudano remembers what Johnny's commanding officer asked her and Joe at the ROTC ceremony: "Just what exactly did you do to raise a boy like Johnny?"

Irene won't take the credit. "Johnny was so gifted," she says. "God gave him everything."

This handsome, athletic young man achieved his goal of becoming a police officer, joining the Niles Police Department in 1977. He served the force with a special sense of dedication. As a judge told his mother, "There are a lot of good men on the Niles force, but Johnny was four cops in one."

Johnny's desire to help other people went beyond the duties of his police work. He loved children, and would go out of his way to help them. Fellow officers tell stories of Johnny using his own money to buy a winter jacket for a teenage boy who had only a windbreaker to wear on a bitterly cold day, and of the time he bought a football helmet for a boy whose family couldn't afford to purchase one for him.

"I'm John, your friend, and I'm a police officer," he'd say each year when he volunteered his time at Big Wheel City, a Niles safety program for youngsters.

Johnny thought nothing of spending his money and his free time to help the youngsters of his community. But in the end, he gave much more. John Utlak gave his life.

On December 8, 1982, Officer Utlak was working an undercover narcotics assignment. Two teenage informants, Randy Fellows and Fred Joseph, Jr., called Johnny and asked him to meet them that night, and to bring money so they could make some big drug buys. Officer Utlak agreed to meet them at 8:00 p.m. in a deserted area near the Gibraltar Steel Company.

The afternoon before Johnny Utlak went to meet the informants, his father implored him to request a transfer out of the undercover narcotics work.

"Johnny, give it up," Joe Sudano said. "Can't you see what it's doing to your mother? She's losing weight. She can't sleep."

As usual, Johnny tried to reassure his worried parents. "I can take care of myself, Dad. I'm a good cop."

"Johnny, we know that," his mother said, "but you can't stop a bullet!"

"Oh, Mom," he said, kissing and hugging Irene, "I'll be all right. I'll stop by around 9:30 tonight."

But by 9:30 that cold December night, Johnny Utlak was dead, shot in the head twice by Fred Joseph, Jr. Johnny hadn't even gotten out of his car before Joseph shot him. His body fell on the snow after his killer opened the car door—the better to rob the dying police officer of the $200 he had brought at the informants' request, his wallet, handcuffs, service revolver, shotgun, and wristwatch.

The murderers even tried to pull the gold chain off of Johnny's neck before they left him to die in the snow. John Utlak's body wasn't found until the next morning, after a passerby spotted a man lying in the snow and called police.

"Murder brings on its own rage," Irene Sudano says. "There's no way to accept any death. But if—God forbid—he'd had a disease and we could have nursed him, we could have given him our love. This way, there was nothing we could do."

Johnny's parents and his younger sister Joanne made it through those first terrible days somehow. Irene remembers seeing her parish priest walk in the door. She had a warning for him:

"Don't you *dare* tell me that this is God's will!"

The priest shook his head. "No, I did not come to say that to you. Irene, it's the evil world. This is not God's doing."

But Irene Sudano was angry at God, and, for a time at Johnny, too, because her loss was so great. "We were so close. We'd sit and talk over a cup of tea about books we'd read, movies we'd seen. And Johnny's sister, Joanne—she lost so much. They were partners in crime when they were growing up, and mentors, and best friends."

Joanne Sudano, 16 at the time of her brother's death, is now an auditor for the Department of Defense. She plans to marry soon. But she and her mother worry about how they'll get through the wedding ceremony without crying for Johnny, who would have wanted so much to be a part of this special day in his little sister's life.

"I took Joanne to try on her wedding dress, and I asked God to give me strength not to spoil it for her. But when they put the gown on Joanne, I cried my heart out. At least I did it with dignity, if that's possible. I just keep asking myself, 'How am I going to make it through her wedding—there in the beautiful church where Johnny's casket lay in the aisle?'"

Like anyone who has lost a loved one, Irene Sudano has asked "Why?" many times over. The answers to her questions just don't add up. What motivated Johnny's killers? They wanted to rob him. Why did they decide to kill him? During the long, painful process of the trial, a witness testified that one of the murderers had said he'd like to kill *all* policemen. Why? No rational person can possibly understand such a desire.

A loving son, Johnny had sent his parents a card on November 2, a little over a month before he was killed. There was no special occasion. The card was an expression of his gratitude to his parents—one of many affectionate messages Johnny's family members received from him.

"I feel the card was saying good-bye," Irene told a

reporter in the months following Johnny's death. But it's hard to say good-bye to a man like Johnny, and Irene Sudano says she never will.

"Your 'whys' will never be answered," she said. "You just have to keep on living the best you can."

Irene and Joe have attended several of the annual memorial services held in Washington, D.C. to honor law enforcement officers who died in the line of duty the previous year. At the first service, in May 1983, Irene found a sense of belonging with other mourners: "We all had the disease—like a leper colony." But there was—and is—comfort in sharing the good memories and the painful times with other survivors of police officers.

Since Johnny's death, both his family and his community have rallied to carry on his tradition of caring. The Niles Police Department established the John A. Utlak Memorial Fund, which helps support Special Olympics and other programs for children. Joe Sudano and other family members formed a bowling team that raises money for Johnny's Fund.

And Irene Sudano reaches out to help those who—like her—have known the agonizing pain of losing son or daughter, husband or wife, father or mother through line-of-duty deaths. For years, she has extended a supportive hand, an understanding voice whenever she could.

"They'll tell me, 'You helped me so much,'" Irene says, "But I was doing it for my son and for all his fellow slain officers. And they helped me, too."

Irene also traveled to Washington to testify before Congress on the need to increase death benefits for police survivors. Her efforts, along with those of many other survivors, succeeded in getting the death benefit doubled. "This was a great, great accomplishment for me," she says.

Shortly after Irene Sudano returned from her lobbying trip to Washington, she was amazed to look out her living room window one day and see an enormous arrangement of wildflowers making its way up to her front door.

"It was so big, I couldn't even see the person who delivered it!" The card read, "Something to show our thanks, appreciation, and love for all that you have done for us. The guys at the station, Niles Police Department."

Today, Irene is eager to see the Law Enforcement Officers Memorial completed. "I am so happy that finally the Memorial will be there. After the death, the shock, grief, the most important thing is to never let them be forgotten. This is the main thing—to respect them for the supreme sacrifice they made."

Johnny Utlak had served five years and three days on the Niles Police Department before he was killed—not long enough. He will never be forgotten by his family or by the many people he helped.

After Johnny's death, his mother received a note from an elderly lady. "You don't know me," she wrote, "but I knew your son, and I wanted to tell you that I am going to miss him so much. He would check on me all the time. If I needed milk or bread, he would go to the store for me."

Ordinary citizens benefit enormously from the small and large sacrifices of men and women like Johnny. The least we can do is say a final, permanent "thank you" to those who have given their lives to serve us. And that's exactly what the National Law Enforcement Officers Memorial is designed to do.

Officer Richard Miller
Baltimore City Police Department
Baltimore, Maryland

◆◆◆

DREAMS LOST, NIGHTMARES FOUND

"Who do you think it's worse for, me or you?" Karen Adolfo asked Betty Miller.

Betty thought for a moment, then said carefully, "I'll have to think about that before I can answer you." The two women had become friends because of a tragic bond they shared—the loss of their husbands, both

28

officers in the Baltimore City Police Department, at the hands of vicious criminals.

But the similarity in their stories ended there. Karen was just 21 at the time of Vince's death. Childhood sweethearts, they had been married only two years. They never had a chance to start the family they had dreamed of. Betty and Dick Miller had been married 31 years. Their two children—daughter Pat, 29, and son, Rick, 30—were out on their own.

A study by Concerns of Police Survivors, funded by the National Institute of Justice, indicates that Karen might have a harder time recovering than Betty: "Younger women, especially if married for 10 years or less, were found to have a more severe reaction to the death of a spouse than the older women married for a longer period of time."

Betty agrees. When she finally answered Karen's question, she said, "At least I had 31 years with Dick. We raised our family together. I have the kids and the grandkids. You have nothing. It's got to be a lot harder."

To an outsider, Karen's question might sound self-pitying or idle. But it was part of her attempt to make sense of something completely senseless, the slaying of her handsome young husband in a Baltimore alleyway on November 18, 1985.

Early that evening, Officer Adolfo noticed a silver Cadillac Coupe de Ville cruising a Baltimore neighborhood. He radioed the dispatcher for information on the car's license tags, and learned that the tags had been stolen from another car earlier that month. Now assisted by a second police cruiser, the young police officer attempted to stop the car. The driver did his best to get away, jumping out of the car to run up an alley, and Officer Adolfo ran after him.

There were three other people in the Cadillac; the second police officer had his hands full with them. So Vince Adolfo was alone when he ran up Iron Alley, where he met his death.

Flint Gregory Hunt shot Vince Adolfo in the chest. Vince died in surgery at Johns Hopkins Hospital shortly after the shooting.

From that moment, Karen's life became a nightmare that has only begun to fade now, almost four years later. Vince's things are where he left them in the home he built for them. Every day, Karen walks past his bathrobe, hanging on the bedroom door where he left it. His clothes are still in the bureau, his uniform in the closet. Still fiercely loyal to Vince, Karen won't hear of dating anyone else.

"I don't know what they mean by letting go," she told *The Baltimore Sun*. "He's so strongly a part of my life. I'll never let go."

In a lengthy interview in the fall of 1988, Karen described her days as tasks to be gotten through, because she knows she's supposed to. Though she dutifully attends to them, her job, her hobbies, her friends do nothing to alleviate the agony of Vince's absence. Only babysitting for her nieces and nephews brings a spark of happiness to this pretty young woman's heart.

For Karen, Betty Miller has been a lifeline, someone who understands her deep, lasting grief, someone she can talk to about Vince without fear of being told "It's time to get over it."

Betty understands too well the pain Karen is going through. On the afternoon of June 12, 1986, her husband Dick, a 31-year veteran of the Baltimore City Police Department, went to his regular detail at Baltimore's Memorial Stadium. For years, Dick spent summer evenings directing traffic when the Orioles baseball team played home games. He loved the team, and had many friends among the players. Betty even found a picture of Dick and Orioles star Brooks Robinson in his wallet after his death. He loved his work so much, in fact, that he passed up his scheduled retirement in January 1986.

"What about that retirement?" Betty Miller asked her husband.

"I think I'll just work one more season with the Orioles," her husband replied.

Betty Miller doesn't waste time thinking "If only Dick had retired when he was supposed to." "It was meant to be," she says matter-of-factly. "That's the only way I can look at it. Otherwise, I'd go crazy."

Dick was directing traffic on 33rd Street around 6:00 p.m. that June evening when a call came over his radio from the east side of the stadium.

"Stop the little white car," the officer said. The caller apparently did not know that the little white car had already tried to run over Officer Michael Parks on his way down from the stadium's east lot.

Dick and fellow Officer Paul Aires went out into the street to flag down the car. They spotted the car, then saw it accelerate. In a horrified moment, Paul said to Dick, "He's not stopping, let's bail out."

The two men ran to the opposite side of the street,

retreating behind a series of traffic cones. But the driver deliberately turned the car to his left. He maneuvered through the traffic cones to get to the officers. His car brushed Paul Aires, but it hit Dick Miller full-force at 55 miles per hour, throwing him onto the hood of the car. Then he hit two more cars, catapulting Dick onto the street.

The driver, Leonard Cirincione, hit Dick with such force that the officer's glasses were embedded in the hood of the little white car.

As Dick lay bleeding in the street, and in the months to come, Cirincione would claim that it was just a little accident. His attitude so enraged Paul Aires that fellow officers had to struggle to keep him away from the suspect.

Under the care of the Chief Physician for the Baltimore Police, Dick was taken to the city's Shock-Trauma Unit. In the hours immediately following the incident, doctors had to decide what to do with Dick's crushed legs. The next morning, Betty signed a permission form so doctors could amputate his right leg. "If they didn't do it, he wouldn't live 48 hours. They thought they might be able to save his left leg, but they didn't know."

Betty saw Dick in the Critical Care Unit that morning. He was heavily sedated. "He didn't look like himself," she remembers. "All the bones in his face were broken. They had to do a trach to keep him breathing. You couldn't really talk to him. We knew he had suffered brain damage, but we never knew how much."

Valiantly, Betty did her best to encourage her husband, who showed little response to stimulation.

"I would hold his eyes open with my fingers and talk

to him. If I told him to squeeze my hand, sometimes he would do it. One day I took in a picture of our grand-daughter and I held it in front of his face. 'I don't know what you're doing in there, but you're sure not making much effort,' I told him. 'If you know who this is, squeeze my hand.'"

Dick stared at the picture for a long time. Tears rolled down his face, and he squeezed his wife's hand.

"Things seemed to be on an upswing for a while, but I didn't want to get my hopes up," Betty said. "On July 3, our daughter was married. She cancelled the wedding she had planned and got married at the courthouse. Later that very day, Dick's condition began to go slowly downhill."

The massively injured police officer suffered kidney and liver failure. Then he started to suffer seizures.

"The seizures still give me nightmares," Betty says. "I've never seen anything like that. They would come every minute. You would see his toes start to shake and then it would get worse and worse—over his whole body. They had to strap him down or he'd be on the floor."

Sunday, July 13, the seizures came even more frequently. At times they were just 40 seconds apart. The doctors were stumped. The anti-seizure drug they were giving Dick could not be prescribed in higher dosages without danger of it killing him.

The ordeal dragged on. Betty and her children kept up their vigil. One night, as they were leaving the hospital, Pat asked her mother, "Why can't he die?"

Betty said, "I can't answer that, but I don't think we'll have to wait too long for an answer."

A practical person, Betty wanted to be prepared for Dick's death. She wanted to buy a burial plot and start making the many arrangements that would need to be made. "If he didn't need it, fine. If he did, I'd be ready." She called one of the doctors treating Dick.

"I need answers," she told him. "I'm not the kind of person who can leave things hanging, and there are things I need to do if Dick's going to die."

The doctor replied that he had no answers to give her.

"Don't tell me you don't have them!" Betty said. "You deal with the worst injuries that can happen to people. You must have an idea of what Dick's chances are."

"I can't tell you," he said.

"I asked you a point-blank question," Betty said. "There are things I have to deal with. How long?"

"If I had to guess," the doctor finally said, "I'd have to say within a week."

"Okay, fine," Betty said. She hung up, called the cemetery, and made an appointment for Monday morning.

Dick died that Monday at 3:05 a.m., 39 days after Leonard Cirincione ran him down. It was July 21, one day before the 32nd anniversary of his joining the force.

Dick was given a hero's funeral, the kind of funeral police are famous for. Thousands of officers attended. Baseball players from the Orioles team paid their respects. And though the pain was deep and lasting for Betty Miller, it comforted her to know that, given the existence of a Leonard Cirincione on that June evening at Memorial Stadium, Dick would have wanted it this way: "Dick would have wanted it to be him who was hit instead of the people on their way to the ball game."

Dick has been remembered with love and appreciation by many. "He was an inspiration to a lot of us younger fellows," Officer Andrew Giordano told the *Evening Sun* just after Dick died. "Whenever the situation around the stadium started getting stressful and we younger guys were losing our patience, we'd just look to Dickie Miller who was cool and calm."

Several of Dick's many friends made sure he had his favorite beer and Hershey Kisses right nearby: They put a supply in his casket. Occasionally, Betty still finds a can of beer behind the flowers on Dick's grave. He has been awarded the highest honors the police department and civic groups can bestow. But perhaps he would be proudest of the plaque erected in his honor at Memorial Stadium. It reads as follows:

In recognition of his faithful service
as a Member of the Police Department
of the City of Baltimore
this tablet is erected in memory of
Police Officer Richard Miller
Traffic Division
Born April 20, 1931
Appointed July 22, 1954
Killed in the execution of his duties
July 21, 1986
His service honored the department.
This plaque is donated by
the Baltimore Orioles Foundation
and the Traffic Division of
the Police Department.

The plaque hangs at the Stadium offices with only two others—one in honor of Baltimore Colts football star Johnny Unitas, the other in honor of Dick's good friend, Brooks Robinson.

For Betty, going through the trial of Leonard Cirincione was maddening. Cirincione, a 29-year-old part-time construction worker, had a history of drug abuse. At the trial, he testified that he had smoked seven or eight joints of PCP, a hallucinogenic drug, the day he killed Dick. The son of a former police officer, he seemed to have a virulent hatred of police, having been arrested twice previously for assaulting an officer. He showed no regret for what he had done. Indeed, the entire Cirincione family professed not to understand what all the fuss was about. They made an obscene gesture at the Miller family in the hall of the courthouse, and Leonard's father stated on a radio talk show that "it was just an accident."

Furious, Betty Miller called the radio station the next day. "Mr. Cirincione," she said on the air, "your son killed my husband. He destroyed my life. I ask you to look in the mirror and see me. I'm like you. You're lonely, but I'm lonely too. At least you have the option of going down to the Maryland State Penitentiary to hug your son and make sure he's okay. My children and I visit the cemetery."

Cirincione was convicted of first degree murder in the death of Richard Miller, first degree attempted murder of Officer Aires, and assault on Officer Papks. The first two sentences are running consecutively. Cirincione is now serving life plus 20 years at the Maryland State Penitentiary.

There's some measure of satisfaction in knowing that her husband's killer is behind bars, says Betty Miller, but it will never ease her pain completely. "I live with this every day. Nobody wants to hear it. People say, 'It's been three years and you should be past it.' Friends we had together aren't friends now. They can't handle it. There's only a few that can look me in the eye. The rest look past me."

"One day, that cemetery looked real good to me." But Betty Miller has gotten on with her life. "It's a struggle to do that. My grandchildren are my life now." The little ones keep her going, as does her involvement with other police survivors through COPS. "If you can reach out and help somebody else, you will get on with your life. You'll never get the answer to 'why,' but you can go on."

Betty Miller keeps Dick's mementoes in a beautiful glass breakfront in her immaculate living room. There, a visitor can see his hat, a baseball, a baseball glove given to Dick by pitching great Jim Palmer, and a host of honorary medals and plaques. Saddest, perhaps, is Dick's badge, with the enamel scraped off in places by the force of the impact of the little white car.

In spite of all her pain and loneliness, Betty is convinced she has it better than Karen Adolfo, deprived so early of so much love, so much potential, and a life the two young people had planned together since they met in their teens. "But she'll make it," Betty says. "Karen's going to be all right."

In a spirit typical of law enforcement officers' survivors, Karen and Betty are trying to help each other make the best of what life has cruelly handed them.

Their efforts heap even more shame on the heads of two murderers who are not sorry for what they did—senselessly killing two dedicated law enforcement officers, men noted for the kindness and respected for their courage. The tidal wave of pain caused by their criminal deeds has not ebbed, not yet. Probably Karen and Betty would quietly tell us that it never really will.

"TALKING ABOUT IT IS PAINFUL. SILENCE IS MORE PAINFUL."

—A participant at a COPS grief seminar.

"After Dan was killed," Pam Gleason said, "some people said to me, 'Well, at least you expected it. You knew what you were getting into when you married him.'

"But Dan's death was not part of the deal!"

Law enforcement officers and their families tend to put the possibility of line-of-duty death out of their minds, simply in order to survive. "You can't think about it," many widows have told me. "You can't let yourself, or you'd go crazy."

But even if you could dwell on the ultimate dangers of the job, there's no way to prepare yourself for the sudden, violent death of a loved one.

"The days after Kevin's death were so hard. It's like this big hole in your stomach that doesn't fill up," said Judi Welsh, whose husband, Kevin, a Washington, D.C. police officer, drowned while trying to save a woman who had thrown herself into the Potomac River in an attempted suicide.

Anyone who loses a spouse, child, parent, sibling, or close friend will experience profound grief. But the survivors of law enforcement officers who die in the line of duty can undergo a host of troubling symptoms, known collectively as Post Traumatic Stress Disorder (PTSD). Combat veterans, hostages, rape and assault victims, and survivors of natural disasters often experience this syndrome, and so do at least 59%* of survivors of police officers killed in the line of duty.

PTSD sufferers can re-live the traumatic incident for years. Awake or asleep, they experience it repeatedly, replaying their loved one's death in their minds like an irresistible, yet horrifying, movie. Often, they become numb, unable to feel any emotions to the degree they did before their loss. Sometimes they stop sleeping.

Understandably, survivors with PTSD have an increased startle reflex. A noise around the house can make them jump, turning a routine episode into a heart-pounding panic attack. Sometimes they experience flashbacks, hallucinations, and illusions that seem very, very real.

"Six months after the death, you might start to smell his aftershave around the house," says Vivian Eney, who lost her husband Chris in a line-of-duty accidental death. "You think you're going crazy. That's why it's so important to talk with other survivors, to know that you're not the only one experiencing these things—to know you're not alone."

Vivian experienced her first flashback a few years after her husband's death. As often happens, her memories may have been triggered by the weather; her husband was killed August 24, 1984. "I was driving on the Beltway on a beautiful day in August when I felt the blood leave my face. My heart started pounding, and I was crying uncontrollably."

---

*Stillman, F.A., Researcher, Concerns of Police Survivors, Inc., Grant No. 85-IJCX0012, National Institute of Justic, USDOJ.

"Mom, you're scaring me," Vivian's daughter said.

"I'm scaring me, too!" Vivian replied.

When a survivor with PTSD does not receive professional help or peer group support, the suffering can escalate. Substance abuse, broken relationships, lost careers can result. It's almost as if the violent, destructive force of the loved one's death never stops chipping away at their lives.

"Survivors and law enforcement agencies don't usually think of themselves as secondary victims, but that's what they are," says Jim Scutt of the National Sheriffs' Association.

COPS' study of fallen law enforcement officers' survivors has shown that the way a widow, mother, or close friend of the officer is notified of the death has much to do with their ability to recover fully from their loss.

Survivors have many horror stories to tell about notification. Some wives learn of their husbands' deaths on the radio or television before the department notifies them. Some have been devastated by the seeming coldness of the officers sent to deliver the bad news.

Jim Scutt speaks to law enforcement officers on the difficult task of notification. "I tell them, 'It's the hardest thing you'll ever have to do as a cop. But if you're the chief or sheriff of a department, shame on you if you don't go personally to make the notification, and you'd better do it right. Take somebody with you to support the family."

Founded by Suzanne Sawyer, wife of a police officer and immediate past president of the Fraternal Order of Police Ladies Auxiliary, COPS (Concerns of Police Survivors) is working with law enforcement agencies across the nation to improve notification procedures. COPS publishes a widely distributed booklet on line-of-duty deaths that will help agencies prepare for the tragedies they never want to think about. As for now, says one widow, too many police departments know "exactly how far you're supposed to stand from the casket, but how to notify the widow—they don't have a clue."

This important booklet is just part of what COPS is doing to help survivors. Survivors of line-of-duty death interviewed for this book gratefully acknowledged the tremendous work done by Suzie Sawyer—work that has made it possible for them to put their lives back together again. A key part of Ms. Sawyer's healing efforts is the annual COPS grief seminar. Each year in May, during National Police Week in Washington, D.C., COPS coordinates this two-day event for officers' survivors. The seminar is held immediately prior to the National Peace Officers Memorial Day service, which is sponsored each year on May 15 by the Fraternal Order of Police Ladies Auxiliary. Started in 1982 by then-FOPLA president Trudy Chapman and Ms. Sawyer, the memorial service honors officers killed during the previous year.

What happens at a grief seminar? "You find out you're not alone. You find out you're not crazy," participants say. Every survivor interviewed for this book stressed the importance of the COPS "family."

"I went the first year to get help for myself," says Doris Beauregard, whose husband Alain and his partner Michael Schiavina—members of the Springfield, Massachusetts Police Department—were shot to death. "The next year I came back to help the others."

At the COPS seminar, survivors talk, cry, yell, laugh, and feel the strength their common bond brings. Special sessions are held to accommodate the varying needs of the survivors.

"First, we try to fill them with hope at the beginning of the seminar," says Vivian Eney, currently National President of COPS. "We try to tell them that the only way to get out on the other side is to go through the pain. If you try to hide from it, it will catch up with you. And we tell them, 'I'm a survivor, and I'm going to continue to be a survivor, and you can, too.'"

Then the participants can choose sessions suited to their particular needs—sessions for husbands of female officers who died in the line of duty; for survivors of officers whose deaths were accidents; for survivors of officers whose deaths were felonious; for parents, "the forgotten grievers," whose pain may be overlooked while the spouse's and children's needs seem to be paramount in everyone's minds.

And there are special sessions for the children of fallen law enforcement officers—100 of the 600 participants in the 1989 Grief Seminar. This year, an art therapist had the kids draw pictures. Often, their images reveal lingering anger, depression, and frustration. When she sees possible problems represented in a child's drawings, the art therapist recommends that the parent seek counselling for the child, to help him or her deal with the enormous pain of losing Daddy or Mommy.

The seminar also includes a session for co-workers of the dead officers. "Man, this was my partner, and I'm not dealing with it very well" is a typical comment in this special gathering. Traditionally police departments have had a "get tough" attitude about emotions, but burying the grief may endanger the living officer as he or she goes about daily law enforcement tasks.

"The officers are told, 'He's dead, it's over with, get on with your job,' says Vivian Eney. "But it's *not* over. Officers worry that their grief may surface any time, in situations where it might do a lot of harm—apprehending a suspect, for example. Remembering the incident can make you freeze in terror, or get more violent. Or you might simply lose your concentration, which is key to one's ability to do the job."

While fellow law enforcement officers might find it hard to express their emotions when a colleague dies, they almost always make a show of force at the hospital when an officer is injured, and at wakes, funerals, and memorial services.

"I don't know of any other profession like it," says Jim Scutt. "At the Memorial Service this year, it rained steadily the whole time. Even with an umbrella, I was sopping wet by the end of it. But there were thousands and thousands of officers there who didn't even have umbrellas. And they weren't about to leave until that last name had been read, that last sacrifice acknowledged."

Vivian Eney says it's tough for police officers to let down the walls they build up to defend themselves from the stress of their jobs. "You go to a police funeral and you see 5,000 pairs of sunglasses. God forbid anybody should see these men cry!"

Special Agent Jim Horn of the FBI Academy's Behavioral Science Services Division says people can be taught to handle trauma and loss more effectively, not by "toughing it out" but by learning to express their feelings, to reach out to others, and to make a conscious decision to be "better, not bitter:"

"Education got us into this: You grow up, you're big, you don't cry. Education will get us out of it: When we can ask for help, we're really on our way."

The first step is talking. "A Holocaust survivor said, 'Pain has everything to do with silence,'" Jim Horn says. "Survivors need to know their feelings are acknowledged, understood, and accepted. They need to know their experience has been validated by others."

Compounding survivors' grief is the fact that our nation has not made an effort to commemorate the ultimate sacrifices made by their loved ones. "The Memorial is so important because you must have a monument of some kind for that healing to take place," as Agent Horn has learned from Dr. Bessel van der Kolk of the Harvard Trauma Center. "If you don't have a physical one, you might erect one mentally," Horn says, creating Post Traumatic Stress Disorder or other problems in the process. "If you're dying serving other people, that should be recognized. These people deserve more than just a little plot of ground."

And so do their survivors, the men, women, and children who in great numbers have gone on to make the most of their lives, reaching out to fellow mourners and doing what they can to improve the lot of heroes in America's ongoing, undeclared war—the war on crime.

Officer Edward Byrne
New York City Police Department

◆◆◆

OUTMANNED, OUTARMED, OUTGUNNED— THE DRUG WARS IN AMERICA

Something went wrong at the Hurricane Motel. Bureau of Alcohol, Tobacco, and Firearms Agents Ariel Rios and Alexander d'Atri were the cream of the crop, selected from among their peers to serve on the Vice President's Task Force on Crime in South Florida, an elite drug-fighting unit. Ariel Rios left his home base of Connecticut and eagerly headed out to accept his new assignment.

Agent Rios grew up in New York City, received a B.S. degree from the John Jay College of Criminal Justice, and was sworn in as a special agent for BATF on December 4, 1978. Ariel Rios quickly earned a reputation for excellence in undercover narcotics work. "He was one of the best," his superiors and his peers would say after his death.

On December 2, 1982, Agents Rios and D'Atri were working undercover in Miami, trying to negotiate a cocaine buy from Cuban drug and weapons traffickers. In a seedy room at Miami's Hurricane Motel, something went terribly wrong. One of the dealers apparently saw other agents moving in outside the motel to make an arrest. He drew a gun. Ariel Rios moved instantly to disarm him. Special Agent Rios was shot in the face. His partner was shot four times. Ariel Rios died almost instantly. Special Agent D'Atri, though seriously wounded, survived.

The investigation the two agents had been working on brought good results for the Task Force, resulting in the indictment of 17 individuals and the confiscation of five kilograms of cocaine, $82,000, one automatic weapon, five silencers, 20 silencer kits, and 20 other firearms.

Ariel Rios, 28, left a wife, Esilda Morales, and two children, Eileen and Francesco. He was laid to rest in the mountains of Puerto Rico.

In Washington, D.C., the headquarters building of the Bureau of Alcohol, Tobacco, and Firearms is now

the Ariel Rios Federal Building, in honor of this courageous warrior in the crusade against drugs.

They call it an "execution-style" killing. It was fast. It
was sure. It was professional murder, motivated by the
greed of drug kingpins.

Officer Eddie Byrne was a rookie with the New York
City Police Department, proud of his job and eagerly
looking forward to following in his father's footsteps as
a law enforcement officer. On February 26, 1988, he
was assigned to protect a key prosecution witness in an
upcoming drug trial. Eddie was sitting in his patrol car
outside the witness's house when thugs working for a
drug lord walked up and shot him in the head
five times.

Officer Byrne's murder was interpreted by many law
enforcement officials as a clear and simple message
from the drug kingpins to America: "Don't get in
our way."

Eddie Byrne had just turned 22.

She died of her wounds eight years later. Officer Jane
Thompson Bowman of the Columbus, Ohio Police
Department died March 9, 1989. She was 36 years old,
the first female Columbus police officer to die from
injuries received in the line of duty—in a drug raid
shooting eight years before.

The young officer was one of four shot in the drug
raid while serving a search warrant. She had been shot
once when one of the fleeing perpetrators returned and
shot her again. The two bullet wounds to the abdomen

caused severe injuries to her pancreas, liver, kidneys, and intestines. Amazingly, she survived the shooting, though she never returned to active-duty police work. Her husband told people Janie was angry about the shooting mostly because it took her out of the front lines.

Jane Thompson Bowman underwent over 30 operations. She was hospitalized 60 times in the last eight years of her life. Finally, her beleaguered body could endure no more, and her gallant fight for life ended March 9, 1989.

Add Officer Bowman's name to the long list of victims of the ruthless drug dealers who want to take over America.

Cadaver No. 1. Enrique "Kiki" Camarena, 37, was a veteran employee of the U.S. Drug Enforcement Agency, serving in Guadalajara, Mexico. Frustrated by the corruption surrounding him, stymied by criminals who simply laughed in his face, Kiki had requested and been granted a transfer out. But three weeks before his scheduled departure, on February 5, 1985, he went to meet his wife for lunch. He never made it.

For a month, U.S. officials tried to rescue Kiki Camerena, with precious little assistance from the Mexican government. When they found him, he was dead.

Enrique Camarena had been tortured. The violations of his body were unspeakably grotesque. A severe blow to the head killed him. He had apparently been buried in a shallow grave. Then the body was exhumed, wrapped in a plastic bag, and thrown on a village roadside with the body of Captain Alfredo Zavala Avelar, a pilot for the Mexican Ministry of Agriculture who worked for the U.S. Drug Enforcement Agency on the side. Zavala had also been tortured; then he was buried alive.

Red Cross doctors labelled the two decomposing bodies Cadaver No. 1 and Cadaver No. 2. Enrique's remains, telling the horror story of his final hours, were all that was left for his wife, Mika, and their three sons, Enrique, Daniel, and Erick.

From New York to Miami to Guadalajara. To Los Angeles, where drug-selling gangs rule whole sections of the city, and to Portland, Oregon, where L.A. gang members have migrated, seeking an ever more lucrative, untapped drug market. To the big cities and the small towns of the Midwest, the South, New England—in fact, in every part of this country today, drugs are destroying our nation.

Drugs destroy drug abusers—or maybe it's more accurate to say that drug abusers destroy themselves. Drugs destroy youngsters, who at the ages of 9 and 10 years old can earn $500 a day for acting as a drug "runner" or "holder." Drugs destroy innocent bystanders, shot while sitting on their front porches or sleeping in their beds, or robbed at gunpoint for drug money, then killed as an afterthought by people for whom human life holds no special value.

Ultimately, drugs have the power to unravel the fabric of the United States of America.

And this is what our law enforcement agencies are up against—the sinister force of illegal drugs, a force so powerful that law enforcement professionals say it's the top problem they face today.

"Drugs are the scariest thing going," says Jim Scutt of the National Sheriffs' Association, "for two reasons. One, officers are dealing largely with people who are out of their minds on drugs. Two, the first shot fired doesn't kill a drug abuser."

A drug-intoxicated suspect doesn't feel pain the way a normal person does. Without a pain reaction, his body keeps going beyond what would normally be possible. But some drugs do more than anesthetize. Substances like PCP and crack seem to make the users paranoid and violent, and sometimes appear to give them superhuman strength.

Scutt recalls the recent death of his police academy classmate, Corporal Charles Hill of the Alexandria, Virginia Police Department. Cpl. Hill died at the hands of a drug-crazed addict, a man who over the course of a couple of hours had smoked a large amount of crack cocaine. Cpl. Hill died trying to save the life of a hostage, who was later discovered to be a drug dealer.

Brandishing a shotgun, the hostage-taker ordered Cpl. Hill to drop his weapon or he would kill the hostage. As the drama unfolded, a police sharpshooter shot the gunman, a blow that should have been fatal to a normal individual. But the gunman was so drug-intoxicated that even after he was shot, he was able to fire two rounds. One killed Charlie Hill instantly. The second seriously wounded another officer. The suspect was finally killed in a hail of police bullets.

"The rules of the street have changed," says Scutt. "Life has little value."

Worse yet, says Dewey Stokes, President of the Fraternal Order of Police, "Drug dealers and abusers have gone from the defensive to the offensive because of the availability of high-power, rapid-fire weapons—what we call 'drug guns.' They have made stopping, searching, and search warrant execution highly volatile and dangerous tasks for officers throughout the country."

The Fraternal Order of Police supports President Bush's permanent ban on the importation of assault, or semi-automatic weapons, but the organization wants to see a larger step taken—an outright ban on all assault weapons, made abroad or in the U.S.

Dewey Stokes explains the FOP's position: "Some assault weapons will penetrate bullet-resistant vests. And since they release a spray of gunfire, they give the drug criminals a much better chance of hitting their targets. If they're not sporting or hunting weapons— and they're not—why not ban them from general purchase and let the officers be more secure?"

Drugs and drug guns have caused enormous changes in police work in the last 15 years, Officer Stokes says. "Then, armed robbery, burglary, marijuana smokers were the big things. Now you have crack use, rape up all over the country, homicide—especially brutal, sadistic homicides, which are on the increase. I attribute that to mind-altering drugs that produce more aggressive and violent criminals."

During this period of ever-increasing drug-related crime, many municipalities have *cut back* on their law enforcement budgets. The result? Too many law enforcement agencies are under-manned and out-gunned by the drug dealers, who will stop at nothing to protect their unbelievably valuable turf.

The escalating violence is creating a reign of terror,

against which courageous Federal, State, and local officers must battle every day of the year, risking everything, giving their lives as did Agent Rios, Officer Byrne, Officer Bowman, and Agent Camarena.

"When I go to testify before Congress in support of our police officers, sometimes the legislators don't understand why I feel the way I do," says Dewey Stokes. "I tell them it's simple. I've been to many funerals. I've held so many widows and babies and children, and I've told them they would be all right. That's what keeps me going. That's why I'm determined to do whatever I can to help all law enforcement officers and their families."

"We have a society that doesn't support law enforcement's sacrifices like it used to," says FBI Special Agent James Horn. "It's a selfish, self-indulgent society, and nowhere do you see that more clearly than in the level of drug abuse."

It will take a lot to stop the drug plague. More men and women will give their lives in the struggle. The least we can do is let them know that their sacrifices are appreciated, and that's why the National Law Enforcement Officers Memorial is so important to the police community. How can we ask our officers to go out every day and risk their lives, when we don't even commemorate the sacrifices of their slain colleagues?

Our fallen heroes in the drug wars should not fade from memory, and they must not. As members of a decent society, we cannot let them be forgotten.

Patrolman James Wier
Denver, Colorado Police Department

◆◆◆

"MOMMY, WHAT WAS DADDY LIKE?"

Too many children of law enforcement officers will never know their fathers. James Wier's sons are two of them.

On June 3, 1987, Shawn Marie Wier was breast-feeding her infant son, Dustin, at 10:00 p.m., and watching the evening news on television, when her world began to fall apart.

A news reporter announced that two police officers had been shot in Denver, 70 miles away. The broadcast was then garbled by audio problems; Shawn couldn't hear the officers' names, but somehow, intuitively, she knew the incident had occurred in the sector where her husband, James, was on duty.

The phone rang, and Shawn found herself in dream time, where everything moves so slowly. "I walked out into the kitchen and stared at the phone. I made myself answer it, finally."

"Is this Mrs. Wier?" a voice asked.

"Yes," Shawn replied.

"Is this James Wier's mother?"

"No, it's his wife."

"Did you hear about the shooting?"

"Oh my God, was Jim there?"

"He's in the Emergency Room."

"Tell him I love him and I'll be there as soon as I can," Shawn said, hanging up the phone. But it would take her over an hour to reach Denver. And it was already too late for James Wier to hear his wife's words of love.

Preparing to leave her home, Shawn went back into the living room. There, on the screen, she saw her husband on a stretcher, being removed from an ambulance. She saw his legs fall limply off the end of the stretcher, and thought to herself, "He's dead." But there was still an oxygen mask on his face; there was still hope.

The trip to the hospital was the longest ride in Shawn's life. When she walked into the hospital, two police officers pulled her aside, saying, "We'll tell you what happened when we get inside." But all Shawn needed was one look at Jim's brother's face. Before Jim's mother could say, "Baby, he's gone," Shawn knew she was a widow with two fatherless children.

Shawn wanted to see Jim. They took her into the morgue. "All I wanted to do was hold his hands," she remembers. "I walked into the room and they pulled him out of a drawer. They had brown lunch bags over his hands for prints and gunpowder. I couldn't touch them."

Both Jim and his wife were just 25 years old that June evening. They had been married less than a year. Their son, Dustin, had been born just 5½ weeks before. Dirk was 3½ years old.

"You go on automatic pilot," Shawn Wier says. "You have to."

James Wier was killed by a cop-hater, a deranged elderly man named Charles Tarr who flew the American flag upside-down, put signs on his lawn saying "DPD (Denver Police Department) = KGB," and harassed officers with numerous crank calls. That night, he had called police once around 8:00 p.m. Then his wife, Mary, called to tell police to ignore her husband, that he was just drunk. But the dispatcher overheard a scuffle between the husband and wife. To check on Mrs. Tarr's safety, Patrolmen James Wier and Jimmy Gose were dispatched to the house at 40 S. Pennsylvania Street. When they got there, they could see a man behind the screen door with a rifle or shotgun in his hands.

It might have helped if they had known what Mary Tarr knew: That her husband was ready to die. "It's all-out war," he was reported to have said. "It's either them or me."

The officers went for cover, Wier crouching behind a three-foot stucco wall and Gose behind a car, just before Tarr opened fire. James Wier rose up from behind the retaining wall to return fire. As he attempted his third shot, Tarr shot him, fatally, in the head.

"Officer down," Gose shouted over his radio. Back-up units arrived within minutes. Before the mayhem was over, Sergeants Ronald Samson and Peter Diaz were also wounded, Samson seriously. Finally, Tarr ended his "war" by turning his gun on himself.

That afternoon, before James Wier left for work, he and his young family enjoyed a picnic together in their back yard. It started to hail, Shawn remembers: "Jim and I were laughing and kissing each other with this hail falling all around."

Indoors, Jim was holding Dustin, described by Shawn as a "clone" of his father. "He'll do okay for himself," Jim Wier said. "Look at me, I haven't done so badly. I've got a beautiful wife."

When they said goodbye to Jim for the last time, Shawn and Dirk didn't expect him back that night because he sometimes stayed over in Denver because of the long drive. "Since you're not coming home tomorrow, bring me a surprise," Shawn said.

"Bring me one, too, Daddy Jim," Dirk said.

Instead, Jim Wier's family had to learn to cope with his brutal slaying.

"Before Jim died, I felt safe, secure, and happy, and I want that back," Shawn says. It would be a long time before her life would regain some sense of normalcy:

After Jim's death, she was hit with a seemingly endless succession of problems. Her car was stolen. Dustin got sick and required lengthy hospitalization. Driving a rental car while her car was being repaired, Shawn was in an accident caused by a drunk driver; fortunately, both she and the boys emerged without serious injury from the totalled car. Dirk's natural father sued for custody of the child.

In the midst of all of this, Shawn Wier somehow completed a Master's Degree in Communications. But for now, her first priority is her family, and a new life she will start on October 13, 1989, as the wife of another police officer, Patrick O'Connor of the New York City Police Department.

Shawn, active in COPS and many other police-related organizations, met Patrick when both were working for a project called Kops'n'Kids that raises money for police orphans. "You do go on with your life, and I was very lucky to find this wonderful man, but the pain of Jim's death isn't over, and it never will be," Shawn says.

Shawn is surprised to find herself marrying another policeman. "I swore up and down I'd never even date another cop!" she laughs, "But I've never been able to blackball anyone on the basis of their profession. When I met Pat, I told him it would have to be a very special person for me to date another cop. He turned out to be that very special person."

Undoubtedly, Patrick O'Connor has a special under-standing of what Shawn's been through. His father, a New York City police officer, was killed in the line of duty in November 1973.

"We're getting married on October 13. Patrick chose the date because it's 10/13—and in police code, 10-13 means 'officer in distress.' I guess he wants his fellow cops to come and save him from me!"

Shawn looks forward to a new life in New York. Asked if she will worry about Patrick's safety, she says no.

"Pat always says, 'If you worry, you're going to die. If you don't worry, you're still going to die.' I try to remember that."

Shawn Marie Wier, just 25 years old at the time of her husband's death, is a survivor. She will tell Dirk and Dustin about James Wier; she will make sure he lives on in their memories.

Doris Beauregard is making that effort for her children, too. There are pictures of their father, Alain, in each of their bedrooms. He is never far from their minds.

Her son, Eric, was 2½ when his father, a member of the Springfield, Massachusetts police department, was shot on November 12, 1985 and died on November 15. Eric still remembers his dad a little bit. But his sister, Chantal, will have to build up an image of her father from pictures, mementoes, and stories.

Doris Beauregard found out she was pregnant with Chantal one week after Alain's funeral.

"The press was reporting that I was pregnant before I even knew I was!" Doris remembers. One of Alain's fellow officers and friends told Doris that Alain had said he thought his wife was pregnant.

When Doris learned she was expecting, she was numb. "A couple of months before, I'd had repeated dreams that Alain was shot and killed. I'd also had dreams where I saw myself pregnant alongside my sister—but without my husband."

Alain Beauregard and his partner, Michael Schiavina, were shot and killed by a man named Eddie Ortez after they stopped Ortez's car. Ortez later killed himself.

Doris remembers going to Michael's wake, but watching scenes of his funeral on television. She was too weak to attend: Alain, who had survived his wound for a few days, had died the day before.

The community rallied around the families of the slain officers. "But the whole experience was so strange," says Doris, "like being in a dream. On the way to the funeral, I felt like Jackie Kennedy. I'm riding in a limo and there are people lined up all along the street. Something takes over and you're acting out a part. People said I was strong. The reason I could be is that I knew Alain was right by my side."

The City of Springfield erected a memorial to Officers Beauregard and Schiavina, and for all other fallen officers. Every year there is a ceremony at the cemetery for the two men. "It's great to know they're not forgotten," Doris says. The memorial and the ceremony will help her explain to her children who their father was, and what he died for.

"Every year Eric gets more inquisitive about where Daddy is. He asks about dying, and it's really hard to explain to a child, 'Well, your spirit goes to heaven but your body stays here.'" A Christmas T.V. program in which a grandfather died helped Eric understand death a little better.

"I try to tell him heaven's a beautiful place—it's nice and peaceful—and that Daddy's happy there. At the same time, he's watching over you and he'll always be with you."

Doris Beauregard has had her bleak days, her moments of complete despair. "But I had to live on for my two children, for those who made me feel happy, and to smile again. The strength of my family, friends, and all the others who supported me has helped me go on with my life."

Like Shawn Wier, Doris has found love again—also with a man who is the son of a police officer, John Shecrallah, whom she recently married. "John has been most supportive through the events that have taken place since Alain's death. John has given Eric and Chantal all the love and guidance he would give his own children."

Doris says she will never forget Alain: "Alain is gone, but thoughts of him and memories will always be with me, as I have a very special place in my heart for him."

Doris's faith in God helped tremendously the healing process. "Sometimes we ask, 'Why me?' But I just pray that he's in peace and that we're going to make it. In some ways, Alain's death made us stronger. We appreciate more than we did before. We don't take things for granted."

These two courageous young mothers have every right to ask the rest of us not to take certain things for granted, either—especially the supreme sacrifices their husbands so willingly made to make America a little better, a little safer for all of us.

Officer Alexander M. Cochran III
Virginia State Police

◆◆◆

WE CALL IT THE *IN*JUSTICE SYSTEM

The young mother is killed by a crack user in an attempted robbery. Her murderer, arrested for assault just a week before, had been released on $5,000 bail.

The elderly sisters, living together in a country hamlet, are brutally stabbed to death. Their murderer is a convicted killer, out of jail because he came up for parole just a few years after he committed his last felony.

Surely everyone in America has heard horror stories like these. They're far too common. Too many Americans will be touched by violent crime at some point in their lives, despite the best efforts of law enforcement agencies to protect them.

The stories above are just two examples of what many Americans see as the failure of our criminal justice system. In its attempts to protect the rights of the criminal, and in its efforts to cope with a burgeoning prison population, it often overlooks two key concerns: the safety of the public and the rights of crime victims.

For many survivors of law enforcement officers killed in the line of duty, the trial of their loved one's killer is a living nightmare. But the verdict and the sentencing are sheer hell.

"The system makes the aftermath as traumatic or more traumatic than the event itself," says FBI Special Agent Jim Horn. "To go to court opens all the old wounds, and this goes on for months and years sometimes.

"When the perpetrator is not caught, there's never closure," Agent Horn continues. "But even when the perpetrator survives and is apprehended, survivors experience second injury, a resurfacing of the traumatic reactions all over again."

It's difficult if not impossible to accept that the person who deprived you of your loved one will get a punishment that seems to you like a mere slap on the wrist.

Outrage is one reaction—a reaction that's familiar to

Mr. and Mrs. Alexander M. Cochran of Heathsville, Virginia. These bereaved parents are determined to change the "injustice system," at least in Virginia, so that killers of innocent people get the punishment they truly deserve.

Their son's killer will be eligible for parole nine short years after the murder occurred. For them, that's far too soon, especially considering the enormity of their loss.

Their son, Alexander M. Cochran III (known by the family as "Sandy" and by his law enforcement and military colleagues as "Al"), was a Virginia State Trooper and a Member of the Second Air Lift Platoon of the Virginia National Guard. At 27, Sandy was an outstanding law enforcement officer, assigned to patrolling the Virginia section of the Washington, D.C. metropolitan area's Beltway superhighway. In the previous year, he ranked third in his division for drunk-driving arrests. In the six months before his death, he nabbed 42 intoxicated drivers. When the cases went to court, he lost only one, "and that was my fault," he told his father. Sandy was determined to improve his near-perfect record: "That will never happen again!"

As his twenty-eighth birthday on January 23, 1987 neared, Sandy was just about to reach some important goals. The son of a former Air Force jet pilot, Sandy wanted to fly a helicopter for the National Guard unit he'd been with for eight years. His ultimate goal was to fly Medivac for the Virginia State Police, having been an Emergency Medical Technician and Lieutenant in the Callao, Virginia Rescue Squad. He had been taking helicopter lessons in Manassas, Virginia, and soon he would be undertaking his first solo flight.

"I just knew that one day soon I'd pick up the phone and Sandy would be saying 'I did it! I soloed!'" his father Mickey told me. Sandy was also scheduled to receive a promotion to the State Police TAC Team in just four days.

But Sandy never got his promotion, and he never got to fly solo. And his dad never got that proud telephone call. Instead, Mickey Cochran says, "Here I was going along fat, dumb, and happy, and the doorbell rings."

Mickey Cochran will never forget the night of January 15, 1987. At 12:15 a.m., his wife said, "Somebody's at the door." They saw three state police cars in front of the house.

Maybe it was her mother's instinct that told Katharine Cochran what had happened before another word was spoken. "Sandy's been killed," she said.

Her husband's hope held out a few seconds longer. "No, he's just been hurt or something."

Sandy's fellow Troopers confirmed the Cochrans' worst fears.

That morning, Sandy had been assigned to a special FBI anti-drug detail. His regular State Police shift would have started at 3:00 p.m., but his sergeant excused him from it. Sandy spent the afternoon running errands and shopping. He was unloading groceries from his car that evening when his sister Susanne called from Colorado.

They chatted for a while, planning for Susanne's visit on the upcoming weekend. The sister and brother had always been close, sharing among other common interests the family passion for animals. (Sandy had a menagerie in his townhouse—a 14-inch monitor lizard, toads, an iguana; Susanne raises big birds, including macaws.) They finished talking around 9:15 p.m., and one of Sandy's neighbors dropped in for a chat.

The two men stood in Sandy's kitchen for a few minutes, talking, when they heard a loud BAM! BAM! BAM!

"Those aren't firecrackers," Sandy said. Technically, Sandy was off-duty. But, as any law enforcement officer will tell you, there's really no such thing as off-duty. When people need help, you react.

Sandy responded without a second's hesitation. He started out the door, then ran back to get his service revolver. Running out into the townhouse development's shared parking lot and lawns, he saw a woman crouched over a man who had been shot. She was screaming, "Get an ambulance! Get an ambulance!"

Sandy headed to his parked cruiser, apparently to call for help on his radio. The neighbor who had been talking to Sandy reports that at this moment he saw something out of the corner of his eye, a figure moving behind a second-floor window. Maybe Sandy saw it, too, because it seems he was just turning his head when the shot rang out.

A single shotgun blast hit Sandy in the back and the head as he was passing in front of his police car. He died instantly at 9:24 p.m., only nine minutes after talking to his sister.

Within three seconds, the shooter turned and fired again, fatally wounding Army Sergeant Dennis R. Kief, who lived in the townhouse complex. He also shot at an off-duty Fairfax County police officer, who was not hit.

By the time more police officers arrived on the scene, the shooter had created a scene of complete devastation in the usually peaceful neighborhood: Two men dead, one man seriously wounded. They quickly apprehended the suspect, a man named Larry Gill.

Mickey Cochran says the pain of his son's slaying is compounded because there was absolutely no reason for it, no motive any normal person could relate to.

Larry Gill was described by people who knew him as quiet, straight, a man who didn't drink or curse, a Bible-reading hunter who adored his wife. Unfortunately for Sandy Cochran and Sergeant Kief, Larry Gill's wife had decided to leave him that night. Her brother, Gregory B. Jividen, had come to help her move out. Larry Gill shot his brother-in-law first. Jividen lost a kidney because of his shotgun wound.

Why did Larry Gill go on from there to kill two more men and attempt to kill another? The Cochrans will never understand it. But after the initial shock wore off, they expected at least that they would see justice done— capital murder charges, preferably the death penalty or at least three life sentences imposed on Larry Gill.

Instead, Larry Gill got off easy.

Charged with only two counts of first-degree murder, one attempted capital murder (for shooting at the off-duty Fairfax County police officer), and one count of malicious wounding, Gill was convicted on two counts of second-degree murder, one count of malicious wounding, and three counts of commission of a felony with a firearm. The attempted capital murder charge was thrown out.

Gill received combined sentences of 55 years. Under

Virginia law, that means that, with good behavior, he can be eligible for parole in 1996.

Mickey Cochran has puzzled over the jury's decisions many times. "How the jury came up with Murder 2, I'll never know," he says.

Out of their outrage and their anguish, the Cochrans decided to do something about a system that ignores the rights and interests of crime victims. They formed the Sandy Cochran Committee, a group committed to judicial change in Virginia.

"We want to change the parole system, to make it follow the new Federal model established in November 1988—you get a 10-year sentence, you serve a 10-year sentence. And we want to change the laws governing truth in sentencing, so that juries are told exactly what happens in the system once the case leaves the court. Most jurors don't have any idea that a convicted criminal can get 10 years today, yet be considered for parole in something under 30 months."

Mickey Cochran also thinks it's outrageous that juries often have no knowledge of an offender's prior criminal record. "After guilt or innocence has been determined, juries should be given full information about prior record, a victim impact statement, and a clear explanation of parole eligibility date and good time release date. Without this information, there's no way a jury can impose a meaningful sentence!"

Another important initiative for the Sandy Cochran Committee is its effort to establish life without parole as a sentencing option. Life without parole would allow juries that don't want to go for a death sentence to put criminals behind bars with no fear of their release.

The Sandy Cochran Committee has seen some successes. "Now we've gotten the life sentence up to 25 years before parole eligibility, which amounts to about 18 years before they're actually up for parole."

The Cochrans want to see a balance that doesn't exist right now in America: "The criminal has all kinds of guaranteed rights and the victim has few." And, as co-chairs of a five-county Mothers Against Drunk Driving chapter, the Cochrans are also fighting to reform the laws governing drunk driving. Mickey has spoken before the Virginia State Crime Commission, the State Legislature, and various other bodies.

Their efforts on behalf of crime victims have not gone unrecognized. They've been the subject of many newspaper articles, drawing much-needed attention to their causes. And in October 1987, President Reagan invited them to attend the unveiling of his Criminal Justice Reform Act.

The Cochrans' work is very important to them, but they wish they'd never had to get involved with the criminal justice system—at least not because of the murder of their son.

"We feel the system let us down, especially Sandy," Mickey says. That's particularly sad when you consider how ardently Sandy believed in that system, how he gave his life supporting it and protecting others.

When you read what others had to say about Sandy after his death, you get an idea of the huge impact of his loss on his parents, sister, friends, and fellow Troopers and Guardsmen.

The 1987 Yearbook of the 76th Combat Aviation Company of the Virginia National Guard is dedicated to Sandy and another Guardsman who died in a skiing accident. "Sgt. Cochran had been in the National Guard unit for eight years, and he was not only a topnotch crew chief, but you couldn't ask for a finer friend." His friends in the Guard thought so highly of Sandy that they flew to his parents' farm, landing six helicopters in a field next to Sandy's grave in the family plot. They brought the Cochrans a wonderful collage of pictures of Sandy in the Guard.

Sgt. Ken Scott told the Cochrans and Sandy's fiancee, Clare McNeal, "Al shared so much with all of us, and we wanted to give a little of that back to you." His Trooper friends have not forgotten Sandy or his parents.

"The Christmas afternoon after Sandy's death, a State Police car pulled up. One of the local officers came in and spent awhile with us. I thought that was exceptionally nice," Mickey Cochran said.

But though his memory has been honored by hundreds of friends and colleagues, Sandy's absence leaves a hole in the Cochrans' lives that will never be filled.

"Sandy was a comic. He kept 'em all laughing. He was a tremendous mimic, the sparkplug of his shift," Mickey Cochran remembers. But clearly, the serious side was there, too, in his dedication to his fellow man, his community, and his country.

Sandy Cochran's humanitarianism seems to have been a part of his character from an early age. His proud father tells a revealing, poignant story about his eight-year-old son:

"One day my wife was out in the yard, and a neighbor lady came over and said 'I wanted to thank you for telling Sandy to walk my son home from school every day. You know, my boy is little, and he wears glasses, and the other boys had been picking on him, but now that Sandy's walking with him, they leave him alone."

But Sandy's mother had never told him to accompany the boy. The gesture came spontaneously from Sandy's heart, as if he were imbued with a natural instinct for great and giving gestures, an instinct that would lead him to heroic service and an untimely, heroic death.

THERE'S NO SUCH THING AS
A ROUTINE TRAFFIC STOP

Despite the action-packed image of law enforcement work most Americans glean from television and movies, there are many slow hours for most officers, hours spent carrying out ordinary, seemingly hazard-free duties – duties you might consider routine.

But when you're in law enforcement, there's no such thing as a routine task, because any situation can escalate instantly into violence.

New York City Police Detective Richard Pastorella says he gets annoyed when he hears the phrase "routine traffic stop." "There's nothing routine in law enforcement. Each call is different. You are always on the line."

Even far beyond America's drug-ridden inner cities, danger awaits every officer on every shift. Take Robert Banker, for example, a Conservation Officer with the Department of Fish and Wildlife in Christian County, Kentucky. Most people would never think of Bob Banker's job as dangerous. But while their primary duties involve enforcing fish and game laws, Kentucky Conservation Officers also have full police powers. They often work alone and routinely come into contact with citizens legally and openly carrying firearms, raising the potential of violence in any encounter.

Bob Banker knew the risks involved in the work he loved, but he probably wasn't thinking about them that day in March 1987 as he checked the licenses of fishermen at Lake Lacy in southwestern Kentucky. Probably, as he went about his duties, he was enjoying the open air, the beauties of the natural environment he cherished

– that is, until he encountered Eric Burns.

Officer Banker quickly learned that Burns was fishing without a license. Despite Burns' apparent attempt to bribe him, Bob Banker wrote Burns a citation, fining him $62.50. Officer Banker then started walking away. He got no more than 20 to 25 feet from Burns when the fisherman picked up a rifle and shot him in the back.

Dennis Hightower was checking his cattle in an adjoining field when he witnessed the incident. He screamed to try to distract the man with the rifle. He succeeded, putting himself in danger. Eric Burns turned the gun on Hightower.

Fortunately, Hightower was only slightly injured by one bullet that grazed his right arm. For Bob Banker, however, Eric Burns' shots were instantly fatal.

"I could have understood this happening during deer-hunting season, but this just didn't make sense," says Officer Banker's widow, Pamela. Losing Bob has been a devastating blow to the Banker family—not only to Pam and the couple's children, Robert Edward and Melissa, but to Bob's mother.

"My mother-in-law has mentioned more than once that the emptiness just won't go away. As for me, well, after the trial ended, I really felt good – like I could go on. But I'm having trouble doing it," Pam Banker says. After a lengthy but successful effort to prove Eric Burns competent to stand trial, Officer Banker's killer was convicted on several charges, and received sentences that may permit his release in 22 years, at age 53.

"Now they're fixing to go through the appeal process and I'm so scared: Is it never over?" Pam Banker is struggling to create a normal life for herself and her children once again. But she is finding it very difficult.

"Everything's on my shoulders—raising the kids by myself—and the loneliness . . . Robbie helps out a lot but there's only so much a 12-year-old can do, and I don't want to put too much on his shoulders."

Conservation Officer Robert Banker was one of far too many law enforcement officers who step into a seemingly routine situation, only to meet their deaths. Robert Elliott was another.

A Miami County, Ohio Sheriff's Deputy, Bobby Elliott was universally liked. "People called him the Pillsbury Doughboy," says his widow, Tammie. "He was a very good-natured person and he laughed a lot. My attorney even told me he thought Bobby was too nice a guy to be a cop."

Tammie disagrees, though Bobby's kind-heartedness might have contributed to his death. On February 25, 1987, Bobby was guarding a prisoner who had AIDS at Stouder Memorial Hospital in Troy, Ohio. No one really knows what happened, but it appears that the prisoner may have asked Bobby to unshackle him so he could take a shower, and that Bobby—compassionate as ever—may have gone to get the prisoner a towel. Whatever the sequence of the events, Bobby and the prisoner struggled; the room was completely turned upside-down after the incident. Somehow, the prisoner wrestled Bobby's gun away and shot him.

The bullet severed two main arteries in Bobby's liver and lodged in his right kidney. He died six hours later in surgery at Miami Valley Hospital in Dayton, Ohio. He was 36 years old.

Bobby's death even shook some of the inmates at the

jail where he worked. A group of them sent Tammie a letter, telling her how much they admired Bobby for treating prisoners like human beings. "They went out of their way to tell me, 'We're not all like the jerk who killed your husband.'"

Bobby is sorely missed by his wife and children, Rhea, 13 months old at the time of her dad's death, Nathan, who was 3½, and Gloria, Bobby's daughter from a previous marriage, who was 11. He was a hard-working, unassuming, kind man who worked side jobs to give his family a few extras. A skilled carpenter, he made and sold wooden swing sets. Together, he and Tammie restored an old frame house he bought for $50.

Robert Banker and Robert Elliott were the kind of law enforcement officers America is richly blessed with: Dedicated family men who wanted nothing more than to build a good life for their families and serve their communities through law enforcement work. They knew they were risking their dreams when they were sworn in as officers of the law. They knew a quiet afternoon they might even find a little boring could erupt in bloodshed at any moment. But they were willing to take the risks—risks most of us wouldn't dream of accepting.

For their special commitment and their special sacrifice, we owe them a debt of gratitude—a debt we can repay by building the National Law Enforcement Officers Memorial in permanent tribute to them.

Sheriff's Deputy Donna Marie Miller
Hillsborough County, Florida Sheriff's Department

◆◆◆

NOBODY'S FAULT, EVERYBODY'S DUTY

Is an officer less of a hero when he or she dies in a line-of-duty accident? Vivian Eney and hundreds of other survivors say "no":

"Much of society will place the term 'hero' on an officer who dies in a shootout or a drug bust. But those who die accidentally don't get that honor. There are no

NOBODY'S FAULT, EVERYBODY'S DUTY

citations, no plaques. Their death is an embarrassment to the police department."

Vivian Eney knows first-hand about the aftermath of accidental line-of-duty deaths. Her husband, Sergeant Chris Eney of the U.S. Capitol Police, was accidentally killed by a fellow officer during SWAT training with an anti-terrorist unit he helped form.

"It was nobody's fault," Vivian says. But she does fault the police department's handling of the events that followed. Chris's name was released to radio stations before Vivian was notified. Most of the family found out about his death from news broadcasts; fortunately, Vivian did not.

When she arrived at the hospital, Vivian remembers, there were no officials to help her. And in the months following, she had to battle to get the benefits due her and her daughters. It took almost a year to get worker's compensation! Vivian's struggle was reported in an article in *The Washington Post,* which officers pinned up at police headquarters with a note:

"We put our lives on the line every day, and our families are treated like *this!*"

It doesn't seem right, and yet the survivors of accidental line-of-duty deaths often receive this kind of treatment. They learn that the benefits immediately given to the family of an officer who is killed feloniously are *not* necessarily coming to them.

It's a lesson Deputy Sheriff Donna Miller's family learned the hardest way possible.

Deputy Miller and her partner, Deputy Fred Clark, were responding to a call. They were in a hurry: A fellow officer had reported he was under fire at a shooting scene. Travelling at high speed, their car hit a patch of sand on the highway that acted just like ice. The car spun out of control and crashed. Deputy Sheriff Miller, 26, died the next day.

Donna Miller's dad has 30 years under his belt as a Sheriff's deputy. But it wasn't until their daughter's death that the Millers learned a frightening fact:

"Because of a clause in the department's insurance policy, you're not covered if you die in an accident," says Donna's mother, Connie. "Donna was killed in the line of duty but not killed by a bullet, knife, or fists. So the family didn't get a penny. And that's how we learned that if my husband had died in an accident at any time in the last 33 years, he would have left me and our five children penniless!"

Donna Miller's family isn't bitter. In fact, her brother Tony became a Sheriff's Deputy in the year following her death, and Donna's dad is in no hurry to retire. "When you're a police officer, you hang in there until you can't do anything more," says Connie Miller. But their daughter's death has been a stunning blow to this law enforcement family.

"I lost my best friend," Connie says. "We did everything together. We played on a softball team. I coached her in cheerleading. She was such a happy-go-lucky person—she loved to fish, ride on the motorcycle with her dad, water-ski."

Yet Donna had a serious side, too. "She always wanted to be in law enforcement, ever since she was a little girl. When she was in her teens, she worked at the Sheriff's Department a couple of hours every day, and received the highest law enforcement award you can get as a high school student."

Donna, who had served as a deputy for eight years, worked in undercover narcotics for two full years. She had just transferred into the Department's Selective Enforcement Unit when the accident occurred.

Accidental deaths like Donna Miller's and Chris Eney's account for approximately half of all line-of-duty deaths each year. Some accidents are unavoidable, but FBI Agent Nancy O'Dowd warns her fellow law enforcement officers not to fall into the trap of believing they are invulnerable. Her husband Jay, also an FBI Agent, died in an automobile accident in September 1987. They were stationed in the New York City area at the time.

"It was the only day in our entire marriage when we hadn't touched base," she remembers. "Jay had gone to Firearms in upstate New York. When he left that morning, he told the babysitter he would be home no later than 11:00 that evening. But 11:00 came and went. He wasn't home."

Jay had a 60-mile drive to make at the end of a long day of firearms practice. Just three miles from home on a rainy, foggy evening, he fell asleep at the wheel. The car ran off the road and hit a telephone pole. Jay's head hit the steering wheel, taking the full force of the impact.

Nancy, who was two months pregnant with the couple's second child, reached the hospital as the priest was giving Jay last rites. "But because he was in such good physical condition, he lived five days," Nancy says. "Those were the worst five days of my life."

Nancy says the Bureau was behind her 100%. But the fact that she and Jay had never discussed the eventuality of either's death left her uncertain at a time when many decisions had to be made.

"I didn't know what he wanted in terms of a funeral. We'd never thought about it. 'Death? Wills? Who, us?'" Remembering a discussion they'd had about the baptism of their first child, Nancy decided Jay would want a Catholic funeral service.

In the two days before the funeral, Nancy experienced a strange, dislocated sensation. "A thousand people filed in and out, and the last time I had seen many of them was in the receiving line at our wedding. I kept thinking, 'Why is Jay up there in a casket instead of here enjoying himself and greeting his guests?'"

When Nancy looks back on her husband's death, she finds many lessons for other law enforcement officers.

"In Agent's Training, you're given three things: a badge, a gun, and a Bureau car. Sometimes these three things make you think you're invincible. Jay may have thought he was. He was proficient in firearms, very good at what he did. I think he lost sight of the fact that he was a mortal person."

Nancy urges law enforcement personnel to prepare for tragic possibilities *now.*

"I can't emphasize enough how important it is to discuss and think about these things. Life insurance— Jay had very little, I had none. I had difficulty recovering his because he was in the vesting period on his policy. Because I was pregnant and had previously had a Cesarean section, I couldn't get life insurance. I finally got some, but not enough.

"Talk about how you'd like your funeral. Talk about a will. Please take care of it. Your spouse will be left in the lurch without this information, and if, God forbid, something should happen, you will be better off knowing what your spouse wants."

Vivian Eney, Connie Miller, and Nancy O'Dowd all support the building of the National Law Enforcement Officers Memorial, and want to see their loved ones commemorated there. Though Chris, Donna, and Jay weren't killed by criminals, they were carrying out their law enforcement duties when they died, duties that put them in the vulnerable situations that caused their death.

"It's not how they died that's important, it's how they lived," says Vivian. "My husband was a hero. He proved that by the hazards of the job he undertook. It's their willingness to walk out of the Police Academy and strap on that gun that makes them heroes."

Their deaths were nobody's fault. But recognition of their sacrifices is everybody's duty.

VISION OF THE HEART

Detective Richard Pastorella is blind. He has lost 70% of his hearing. Only portions of fingers remain on his right hand.

For Richard, it wasn't always this way. On December 31, 1982, as a member of the New York City Police Department's Bomb Squad, he was trying to safeguard a bomb planted by a Puerto Rican terrorist organization. The bomb exploded in his face.

Detective Pastorella underwent 13 operations to restore his face. "They did it very, very well. I wasn't really permanently disfigured. This gave me the confidence to stand before people and speak, to talk about the plight of police officers."

Today, Richard spends a great deal of time doing exactly that. He cautions his law enforcement brothers and sisters to be careful, to protect themselves. And when they are injured, he musters all the resources of the Police Self-Support Group he founded in 1983, both for the injured officer and for the family.

The Group helps law enforcement officers find a new role for themselves after severe injury. "Most disabled or injured officers were sitting at home with nothing to do before the Police Self-Support Group was founded," says Pastorella. "They were an untapped resource. They still had all this experience, training, and altruism we couldn't put to use any more.

"I showed them they could help their brother and sister officers by giving them moral support and teaching them to take care of themselves. And I think we challenge them. It's as if we're saying, 'If we can manage in this condition, what about you as a whole human being?'"

The Police Self-Support Group can often break through the despondency that frequently follows disabling injury. "Since our organization was founded, three people who attempted suicide are now alive. Without the Group they'd be dead today. Six more who wouldn't have otherwise returned to work have done so. And four are returning to college, so they'll be productive members of society again."

He spoke of a fellow New York Police Department officer who was rendered a quadriplegic by a blast from a teenager's gun. "Steve McDonald said on a CBS news segment that if it wasn't for Richard Pastorella and his organization, he wouldn't have had the will to live," Richard says. "Now Steve's not just living. He's helping other police officers too."

Though Steve McDonald can only move his neck and head, he and his wife Patti Ann are setting an example for the world to see. By appearing on television and radio shows, speaking at meetings and ceremonies, and writing a book (*The Steven McDonald Story*, co-authored with E.J. Kahn III and published by Donald J. Fine, Inc.), they are sending a message that even the most traumatic injury can be met with love, hope, and faith.

Steve's forgiveness of his assailant seems almost super-human to many people. In a remarkable statement to the press on March 1, 1987, Steven's compassion and courage stunned his listeners. At that time, Steven was not able to speak because of his tracheotomy tube, so Patti Ann, fighting back tears, read Steve's statement as the respirator keeping her husband alive made its characteristic noise in the background:

"On some days when I am not feeling very well, I can get angry. But I have realized that anger is a wasted emotion, that I have to remember why I became a police officer. I'm sometimes angry at the teenage boy who shot me. But more often I feel sorry for him. I only hope that he can turn his life to helping and not hurting people. I forgive him and hope that he can find peace and purpose in his life . . .

"I ask you to remember this. I chose the life of a police officer with all its risks. I believe that I am the luckiest man on the face of this earth. I only ask you to remember the less lucky, the less fortunate than I am who struggle for the dignity of life, without the attention and without the helping hands that have given me this life. God bless you all."

Steven's positive attitude in the face of his disabling injury has inspired many. Dewey Stokes of the Fraternal Order of Police believes that Steven and officers like him deserve more of our grateful recognition in return.

"These guys are the forgotten heroes. Had they died, they would have gotten a big funeral, a big check from the Federal Government and maybe the state government, and a lot of public attention. But since they didn't die, they get nothing."

Officer Stokes says there will be more and more officers serving a "life sentence" of severe disability. "We lost 161 officers in 1988. If it weren't for bullet-resistant vests, trauma units, and the good doctors and nurses, we would have lost a lot more. But many of those who are saved are committed to a life within a home, a bed, a wheelchair."

Richard Pastorella is determined to help those officers regain a meaningful role in police work. "My name, Pastorella, means 'little shepherd,' and I believe I am a shepherd. I have been asked to bring back these police officers who strayed from the flock, those who still say, 'How could God do this to me?'"

Despite his unfailingly upbeat attitude, Detective Pastorella has also known despair. "After the explosion, I was bitter, because I didn't understand how God could do this to me. I led a good life, I helped my fellow man, I worshipped every week. I did what I was supposed to do. And look what happened to me. I was an avid reader, and now I couldn't see. I loved music, and now I couldn't hear. I enjoyed sculpting—and now I couldn't hold a hammer in my right hand.

"Before, I guess I'd gotten jaded. You put up walls because you have to. You see people's problems day in and day out, and you build up a facade to protect yourself. But in that explosion, my facade was literally stripped away, and that changed my life totally."

Richard Pastorella has chosen to embrace his new life whole-heartedly. "I like to think I'm a better person than before, because I was able to take my handicaps and use them to my advantage. I can't see with my eyes, but I can see with my heart a lot better."

Now pursuing a graduate degree in psychology, Detective Richard Pastorella is a happy man. "I'm now doing what I should have been doing all along, only I needed a nudge. I wouldn't trade my life today for my life before. I feel good, I'm being productive, I'm help-

ing my fellow man—and that's what I was put here to
do. We *are* our brother's keeper!"

Detective Pastorella shares that guiding principle
with thousands of other brave men and women who
put their well-being at risk every day for the rest of
us—an idea of service demonstrated most honorably
by one of his "brothers in blue," a young man named
Kenneth Wrede.

Officer Kenneth Wrede
West Covina, California Police Department

◆◆◆

"WAY TO GO, MOM AND DAD!"

Kenneth Scott Wrede, a West Covina, California police officer, ran head-on into the diabolical power of drugs in August 1983. While he was writing a traffic ticket, a woman stopped to tell him of a man acting suspiciously nearby.

Ever the dutiful policeman, Kenneth Wrede, 26, an officer for three years, went to investigate.

There he found Michael Anthony Jackson, staggering down the street, walking into bushes. Obviously, all was not right with this man.

Kenneth Wrede walked up to him and started asking questions. The man ignored him, brushed him off. To get Jackson's attention, Wrede tapped him lightly on the back of the legs with his baton.

From that point, it seems, Jackson went into a rage, displaying an anger bolstered by the notorious drug called PCP. He ripped a support stake away from a tree and started swinging it at Officer Wrede. He tore Wrede's badge from his shirt. He kicked at him and hit him. Ken Wrede retreated to his patrol car to call for help from any law enforcement officer in the vicinity.

During the confrontation, Kenneth Wrede tried to talk Jackson out of his fury. "Kenny was always the peacemaker," his mother Marianne says. "Kenny used restraint when he tried to apprehend Jackson, and that restraint cost him his life."

As the altercation continued, Officer Wrede called for help again. But help didn't arrive until after Jackson had reached into the patrol car, ripped the officer's shotgun from its mount – a feat requiring almost superhuman strength—and fired one fatal blast into Ken Wrede's face, right under his eye.

It took several officers, one of them a close friend of Ken Wrede's, and a police dog to subdue Ken's killer. On the way to the police station, Jackson bragged about killing a police officer, though in court he later claimed he had been so "wacked out" on PCP that he didn't remember anything that had happened that day.

Jackson's defense was based on the idea that, because

he was intoxicated with PCP, he didn't know what he was doing, and was therefore innocent. Fortunately, says Marianne Wrede, the jury saw right through it. Jackson was convicted of Kenny's murder and sentenced to die in the gas chamber.

Said Prosecutor John Ouderkirk: "The moral to the story is that you can't get high on illegal and dangerous drugs, run around and commit violent crimes and then say 'It wasn't my fault.'"

Ken Wrede's parents, Kenneth and Marianne, find some comfort in the fact that Jackson received the death sentence. And, unlike many survivors, they found court officials sensitive to their concerns and supportive in the fight to bring Jackson to justice. But any other comfort is hard to find.

"He was just a super kid," says Marianne of her son. Many in the West Covina community echoed her opinion. Marianne and Ken received a special letter after Ken's death.

"This lady wanted to tell me how great Kenny had been with her little girl," recounts Marianne. "Kenny was just passing by right after the child's cat had been run over and killed. He stopped to comfort the little girl." Kenny was so good with kids, in fact, that he was assigned to the difficult and delicate task of interviewing sexually abused children.

To honor Kenny, a grateful community designated a new street "Wrede Way." Spacious, handsome new homes are being built there—"a fitting tribute to our son," the Wredes say.

Kenny's colleagues on the West Covina Police Department haven't forgotten him, either. Chief of

Police Craig Meacham has done much to support the Wrede family: "As far as I'm concerned," Marianne Wrede says, "that man walks on water." Kenny's close friends on the force carry something of Kenny's with them all the time. One officer told Marianne that remembering Kenny's fate may have saved his life:

"The officer was involved in an incident where the suspect pointed a gun at him. Kenny's story flashed through his mind, and the officer pulled the trigger. He told me, 'I don't know if I would have done it if it weren't for Kenny.'"

Like all fallen law enforcement officers, Ken Wrede's death leaves a painful void in the lives of his co-workers and many in the community he served. But his family feels the most painful void of all.

Kenny left a wife, his parents, and three sisters. Since his death, his wife, Denel, went through her own personal nightmare, and she says she will never forget Kenny. She has re-married and had a child, re-building her life in a way that's not possible for Kenny's parents.

Ken Wrede was close to both parents, not ashamed of showing lavish affection to those he loved. His father remembers Kenny taking him on ride-alongs in his police cruiser; Kenny would kiss him on the cheek when he brought him back to the station, saying "See ya later, pop."

Marianne remembers that Kenny wouldn't take her on the ride-alongs. "Mom, how does it look if I have my mother with me? 'Hey guys, I'm bringing my mommy with me in my squad car.'"

For Marianne, the strain of losing Kenny threatened her health, severely aggravating a back problem which forced her to leave her job as an elementary school librarian. Her husband took a year off of work. Kenny's three sisters have suffered greatly, too, and all the family members have sought help through psychological counselling.

But perhaps the best antidote to despair for the Wredes is their involvement in Concerns of Police Survivors (COPS). Marianne was elected President of the newly established California chapter.

"We're constantly writing letters and making phone calls, trying to help other survivors we hear about," she says. "And we're very involved in victims' rights groups. We worked hard to keep California supreme court justices who were anti-death penalty from being confirmed."

Ken and Marianne Wrede could never have dreamed they'd be so involved in so many causes. "We'll be somewhere—at a reception or a meeting—and one of us will look at the other and say, 'Here's another situation your son has gotten us into!'"

They wouldn't have chosen this work, but it has helped them in the healing process. "It's a way of turning something negative into something positive," Marianne Wrede says. And it helps to know that Kenny would have wanted them to choose this path:

"I know if Kenny could, he'd tell us, 'Way to go, Mom and Dad!'"

OF WEEPING ADULTS,
WHO WEAR BADGES

What goes through the mind of a police officer's son or daughter when Dad leaves the house for his shift? In this column, reprinted with permission from Tribune Media Services, columnist Bob Greene brings us close to the heart of a Chicago officer's daughter. Her poem echoes sentiments that are doubtless shared by thousands of young people across the country.

Cops cry.

Years of watching movies and television shows featuring actors portraying unemotional, hardened police officers have managed to convince the public otherwise. But cops cry.

Just last weekend, off-duty Chicago police officer John Matthews was brutally beaten to death, allegedly by five men who had been holding an outdoor "beer party" that Matthews and other officers had earlier broken up. He was attacked so savagely that it took nearly seven hours to identify his body.

Police officers sometimes die in the line of duty; they know that when they apply for the job. On September 22, 1986, Jay Brunkella, a tactical officer in Rogers Park District, was killed during a drug arrest.

I was thinking about Officer Brunkella's death when I heard about this latest killing of an officer—I was thinking about it because I know what happened in the aftermath of Officer Brunkella's death. It says a lot about what goes on inside of all police officers, and inside the members of their families.

Shortly after Officer Brunkella's death, one of his

fellow members of the Rogers Park District tactical unit—Officer Ken Knapcik—returned home after his shift to find a note addressed to him on the dining room table.

"Dad—

"This poem came directly from my heart.

"I love you so much it scares and amazes me that you go out every day and risk everything to provide us with all that we have.

"I didn't write this poem to scare you or Mom, I just wrote to express how lost I'd be without you!

"I love you Dad!" It was signed by his 15-year-old daughter, Laura. Laura added a P.S.:

"Hey be careful out there." With the note was a poem Laura Knapcik had written. Titled "The Ultimate Cop," it was dedicated "To all cops in the world who have daughters who love them with all their hearts. And especially my Dad."

It reads as follows:

He picked me up from school,
his excitement he didn't hold back.
He shared with me his enthusiasm
of our cities' power attack.

Tonight there will be a drug bust
somewhere in an empty lot.
My dad would bust the dealer
and become the ultimate cop.

He dropped me off at home,
he kissed me and held me tight.
As he drove off, he said,
"Say a prayer for me tonight."

At home I went on as usual,
waiting to hear from Dad,
hoping he made the bust,
hoping he nailed them bad.

At 10 I watched the news,
anxious to hear the outcome.
When a newsman read his news
I felt my heart turn numb.

The stern-looking newsman
announced in a voice like thunder.
As my eyes filled with tears,
I said to myself, "Oh why
couldn't Dad be a plumber!"

I screamed at the top of my lungs,
filled with sadness and rage.
I realized then that being a cop
was more than an act on a stage.

Mom awoke with the sound of my screams,
running in fear to me.
Before she could ask, she saw
Dad's body lying dead on the ground.

She fell down on the couch
and grasped for a breath.
She just couldn't cry—
she was scared to death.

I was running like crazy,
throwing things all around
until my mother got up
and tackled me down.

I couldn't stop shaking,
I was nervous and so scared,
I yearned for my Daddy,
and on that thought I blared:

"Oh Daddy, dear Daddy,
where are you now?
I feel so scared and lonely.
Please show me how . . .

to have faith in God
and in your will to live.
Show me a sign that your life
you'll not give.

Daddy, my Daddy,
can you hear me cry?
Oh God, I need my Daddy,
Please don't let him die!!!"

That night Ken Knapcik stood alone in his house as he
read his daughter's note and her poem. He is 40 years

old, a 20-year veteran of the Chicago Police Department.

"I started to read it," he said the other day. "I took several minutes. I would get through a part of it, and then I would have to stop and wait awhile before I could go on. I was weeping.

"She had never told me that she was scared for me. She had told me she was proud of me—but she never told me she was scared. I have three daughters, and I don't recall any of them ever telling me that they were scared.

"I took the poem to work with me the next day and showed it to my fellow officers. I've never seen so many grown men weep. Some couldn't even finish it."

Laura Knapcik told me, "I never told my dad how scared I was, because I didn't want him to feel guilty for being a policeman. One night when I was about 11, I had a dream that he had been killed. He was working midnights when I had that dream, so I got into bed with my Mom. I was still crying; she asked me what was the matter. I told her. She said, 'It is scary.' She said that she gets scared too."

Laura said that ever since she and her sisters were small, her dad had told them that he wished he could carry them around with him. She used to laugh at that, thinking her dad was joking—the image of him carrying the family with him seemed sort of funny to her.

"Then when I was a little older, he and I were having an argument," Laura said. "He said, 'Don't you understand that I'm serious? I wish I could carry you and your sisters and your Mom with me every moment. I wish I could have you with me all the time, so I could always be there to protect you." That night it was Laura who cried.

So, now another Chicago police officer is dead, and this seems like the proper time to tell you the story about Officer Knapcik and his daughter's poem.

The poem, by the way, is not framed in the Knapcik's house, and it is not taped onto a page in a scrapbook.

It is in the pocket of Officer Knapcik's police jacket. He carries it with him every time he leaves the house for a new shift.

"I don't want to be out there without it," he said. "I'll probably carry it with me forever."

Detective John Davis
Phoenix, Arizona Police Department

◆◆◆

"BIG JOHN": A SON REMEMBERS

"That was the heartbreaker—that Dad survived for a while, then died. He was up and walking. I helped him walk. The next thing you know, he's got this bacterial infection that causes him to lose his life."

Rick Davis is talking about his father, "Big John" Davis, a Phoenix, Arizona police detective who died on August 6, 1982, a little over a month after he was shot attempting to apprehend a bank robbery suspect. The suspect also shot Phoenix Officer Ignacio Conchos, who died almost instantly.

Detective Davis had bullet wounds in the thigh and the abdomen. He was doing fine after the first surgery. "Folks were saying to Dad, 'We'll see you in a couple of weeks.' They'd tell him they were going to buy him a beer when he got out of the hospital."

But doctors needed to operate again. And after the second operation, John Davis began to show signs of a bacterial infection.

"He knew after the second surgery that he wasn't going to make it," Rick Davis says. "He would shake his head and wave his hands, because he knew."

Detective Davis's wife, Arlean, and the couple's two sons, John Davis, Jr., then 22, and Rick, then 20, buried the 12-year veteran officer on August 12. Thousands of people along the funeral procession route paid their respects to John Davis, says Rick: "I knew that he was well-known—to see all the people lined up on the side of the streets. Even the street people were taking off their hats. People were praying. It made me feel good to know how many people understood what we had been through."

Rick, a college student on a basketball scholarship at Oklahoma Baptist University, had to return to school less than a week after his father's death. It was tough, but Rick worried that it would be even tougher for his mother, brother, and 3-year-old nephew, who had to stay in Phoenix with the ever-present memories of their husband, father, and grandfather.

"When I got back to Oklahoma, nobody knew about

my dad's death. They'd ask me, 'How was your summer? Did you have a good time out there in the sun?' And I'd have to explain the whole thing."

It was a terrible year for Rick Davis. "I flew home three times before Christmas to check up on Mom. I wanted to go back to my family, but I was on a basketball scholarship. I had to stay. I couldn't afford to pay my way through college."

People had said Rick Davis was going to be a big star. But that season, he averaged only 10 points a game. Before his father's death, 30 to 40 points per game was routine for him.

"Dad's death blew away a lot of stuff. Nothing really helped," he said. "By the end of the season, I was the last one on the bench, watching. It really hurt me. I kept worrying about whether I should have stayed home." Somehow, Rick managed to keep his grades up. The next year, he transferred to Grand Canyon College in Phoenix. "John Shumate gave me a scholarship there. He was one of the first coaches to win over 20 games in his first year. I did really well that year. It made me real happy to be able to play in front of my mother."

Rick graduated from college in 1985 and got a job in TV, "thanks to the Phoenix Police Department. I took a course that required my interviewing people in the communications field, so I went to the Media Relations person at the Police Department, Brad Thiss, who had known Dad." Thiss took Rick around to the local TV stations. KTSP-TV offered him a job as a part-time editor. Today he is a photographer for the CBS affiliate.

When I talked to Rick Davis, he was groggy, having been up till 4:00 a.m. the night before, covering a police shooting. "Being a photographer puts me real close to Dad's work," Rick says. "I see a lot of violence." Rick had even applied to be a police officer in 1985. Though his father's old police friends encouraged him, his mother "was not too thrilled about it." Rick decided to stay with the television station.

Rick Davis still misses the father who meant so much to him. "He did a lot for us. He taught me to play basketball, and that helped me get a college education. He taught me and my brother how to deal with things.

"One time, he told me to go get something at the store. I went to get in the car, and the spark plugs were missing. He'd taken them out so I could learn about taking care of cars. I went back to him and said, 'I need some money. For some reason my spark plugs are missing.' Dad gave me the money, then watched me fix the car."

For a long time after his father's death, Rick suffered flashbacks every time he saw a police officer. "One time in the gym at college, there were a couple of cops. I stood and stared at one of the guys. A girl came by and asked me why I was staring. I said, 'He's wearing a bulletproof vest.'"

Rick explains that his father, a plainclothes detective, rarely wore a protective vest. "A lot of the older guys didn't," he says, "it almost seemed like a seniority kind of thing." Seven years after John's death, Rick still seems to wrestle with the fact that John Davis might have survived, had he been wearing the vest.

Not long ago, Rick went with a news crew to cover yet another police shooting. The officer, Johnny Chavez, had been shot in the heart—but, unlike John

Davis, Chavez was wearing a bullet-proof vest. "Man, I was nervous. I was so glad to see he wasn't killed. I shook his hand."

Rick Davis doesn't identify himself as the son of a slain police officer when he's with police officers as a photographer at the scene of a crime. "For me to try to identify myself that way would change their attitude toward me as a photographer completely. But I like to be there. I like to help them out in any way I can."

Big John Davis would be proud of this son who had to finish growing up without him.

WHY DID THIS HAVE
TO HAPPEN TO ME?

Every day, law enforcement officers deal with life and death. It's part of the job, and it's why the job's so difficult. This book includes many stories of officers who died in violent confrontations with criminals. But death and injury are not the only traumatic outcomes of such altercations.

The following account, written by a veteran officer of a federal law enforcement agency, describes what can happen to an officer who must kill to protect himself or others. It is a moving example of the extraordinary stress peace officers must come to terms with.

The question always was, "Why did this have to happen to me?" And I guess I will explain that question a little later.

The newspaper headline was titled "Federal Agent in Fatal Shootout." The United Press International carried it. It said, "a federal agent shot and killed a man in a downtown gunfight on Friday. Local police have identified the agent but were unable to say who the dead man was, because he was carrying three different identifications.

Well, I was the federal agent the newspaper described, and I remember the incident as though it were yesterday. I remember seeing the gun emerge from behind the guy's back in his left hand, I entered the dream world of a slow-motion movie. This guy, who only moments before had been standing a few feet from me, was suddenly an actor in a frame-by-frame B movie edged with a kind of soft, fuzzy fog. I could only see that gun and his big, brown, watery eyes that seemed to be laughing at me and saying, "I've got you now!"

"I ain't goin' nowhere with you," he was saying in that deep, slow voice of a reduced-speed audio tape.

I knew the gun had to be a toy as the frames slowly clicked by and the gun began to level off at my chest. It just had to be a toy. There was just no way that somebody would shoot me—a federal agent.

"Drop it!" I tried to scream at him, but my mouth wouldn't work. The frames kept clicking silently by in this dream world with no sound.

"I can't take a chance," I said to myself. "If he points it at me, I've got to shoot." Suddenly my service revolver was in my hand and I felt myself moving in slow motion to my right as I tried to get to the outside of his gun hand.

"Was that a puff of smoke from his gun barrel," I thought, "or part of the fog in my movie? Okay, what's in your field of fire? What's behind him? Okay, it's a brick wall. Nothing on the left. Nothing on the right. Calm down. Take a breath."

In my mind, I painted a rectangular target outline on his chest. "Just like at the range," I thought.

I took one last look into his eyes as I felt his slug pass by my left hip . . . and fired twice. I could see his expression change as I watched my first round impact on his chest.

"I guess you've got me," his eyes said, and I literally saw into his soul as his eyes rolled back, and he was knocked off his feet. Though he was on the ground, the target outline was still suspended in midair, and I had to shake my head to make it disappear.

"Oh my God, what have I done?" I thought, as the wave of nausea swept over me, and I began to vomit on the sidewalk at his feet. My movie was suddenly real time, and I could hear all of the running and screaming by those who had witnessed this terrible thing. It was strange because my ears weren't even ringing. I leaned down, moved his gun away from his head where it lay, rolled him over on his back, and heard one last, noisy exhalation. There was no carotid pulse to be felt.

"Finally over," I thought, and I started to cry. I vomited my way into a store and called the boss. I was sobbing so hard that I had to tell him three times before he understood what I had done. When I came back out, I breathed a deep sigh of relief that his gun was still there. I was sure somebody would have taken it.

I knew the manual said to handcuff him, but it just didn't seem right. It would look as though an execution had taken place here. Suddenly, I realized that the wall I had seen behind him was really a floor-to-ceiling window with the curtains drawn. I wasn't sure where my second round had gone and frantically searched that window for a bullet hole. I asked bystanders if anyone else was hurt and was assured that only the bad guy had been hit. Later, I learned that my second shot hit him in his left side as he was pivoted by my first round. I begged them not to leave so the police would have witnesses to verify my story.

The next few hours were a blur of time. I was numb and frightened. The local police were great. They got me out of there before the news crews could photograph me and bought me some of my favorite cigars. We drove around the city for the next couple of hours while the two police officers tried to console me. Finally, the radio crackled, "We're ready for him."

Homicide Division did an excellent job of protecting me from the press and well-wishing officers. My boss was already there, and I could tell he wasn't real happy. An hour later, my taped statement was finished, and I walked back to my office to dictate my personal statement to be submitted with the inspection report to headquarters.

The next two weeks were a numbing blur of events as I told my story over and over to the inspectors from headquarters and anyone else who wanted to hear the gory details. I just could not be consoled in my guilt over taking a human life. Some of the comments people made were well-intentioned, but unbelievably insensitive. The inspectors chastised me for being so emotional during my taped statement to the police. Congratulatory remarks seemed especially inappropriate to me. Then there was the white police officer who congratulated me for "bagging my career nigger." His remark certainly did not reflect my feelings. So many of the people seemed to be living vicariously through my experience. They were sucking me dry and giving nothing in return. They wanted to hear everything of the excitement but nothing of my emotional trauma.

I got a brief emotional respite four days after the shooting when the county prosecutor advised the press that I "was justified in using his firearm . . . to protect lives and property" and that there would be no case presented to the grand jury. I waited for similar words from my own agency, words for which I would wait nine and a half years.

On the fourteenth day after the shooting, I was walking back to the office from the cigar store when it suddenly hit me: I had almost been killed! I couldn't breathe as the anxiety gripped at my throat and locked me in a bear hug. I was barely able to make it back to the office where I locked myself in my work area and tried to regain control.

Over the next six months, I began to lose my short-term memory: I kept losing my car keys. I lost my train of thought in mid-sentence. I became enraged when I couldn't remember where I had left my checkbook. The nightmares intensified and came several times each night. It was always the same: There was my bad guy standing at the foot of my bed smiling at me with a gun in his hand. I reach for my gun; six good shots in his chest, reload, six more shots, and he's raising his gun to fire when I wake up screaming. My constant question was always: "Why did this have to happen to me?"

My crying spells always seemed to come at the most inappropriate times. I was drinking more and more. Rarely was I sober. I came to work drunk, usually drank my lunch, and went home drunker still. My production statistics dropped from many arrests and cases closed to no arrests or cases closed for many months. For the first time in my marriage, I was unfaithful to my wife. I thought I was slowly losing my mind. Surely "they" would send me away.

I made life a living nightmare for my wife, who could not understand my emotions. She lived with her anguish by denying that "it" had even happened. If nothing had happened, then there was nothing to discuss at home, and the shooting became a forbidden subject. It became the turning point in a marriage that soon started a downhill slide to divorce seven years later.

After seven months, I realized I couldn't keep killing myself. My parents and siblings had slowly recovered from their initial shock but felt helpless as they watched my continuing self-destructive behavior. Several local police officers who had been through similar incidents were finally able to help me see light at the end of my tunnel. My father, a minister, was my closest friend throughout the whole ordeal. I think the incident may well have forced him to evaluate many of his personal feelings and religious beliefs. I stopped drinking and slowly resolved my fears and guilt with their help.

The nightmares slowly diminished and eventually stopped two years after the shooting. But I swore I would neither forgive nor forget my agency for what "they" had done to me and the lack of support I had received from "them." My boss had been involved in a shooting several years before and felt I should work it out on my own. At no time did anyone from management even tell me that I was right, that my agency felt the shooting was justified. For me, I never had "closure" or an end to my incident. The stigma was there: He . . . is a "killer." Several transfers later, I was still the problem child and trouble-maker for my supervisors. I had a chip on my shoulder for management that was the size of a giant sequoia. I felt that all of my problems were their fault.

In February 1988, the employees assistance program of my agency required me to attend a critical incident seminar along with twelve other agents who had been involved in critical incidents during their careers. I was skeptical, and I wanted to stay mad.

At the end of this seminar, I emerged without my nine and a half years of bitterness, frustration, anger, and rage. Police Psychologist Roger Solomon, who was then with the Colorado Springs Police Department, Special Agent Jim Horn of the FBI Behavioral Science Services Unit, and this group of my peers had helped me to finally unload those Herculean chips from my shoulders and rid myself of all that emotional baggage.

The head of our agency addressed us during the third day of that seminar and committed headquarters support to ensure that those mishandled incidents from the past would never be allowed to happen again. Those three days filled me with an inner peace that I've never experienced before. After nine and a half years, I had finally received the vindication and approval from my peers and the management of my agency that I had always wanted and needed. I can now get on with my life.

In retrospect, it was my vulnerability and the feeling of a lack of control that did me in. I hated that guy for what he had done to me: for showing me my vulnerability and taking control of my life away from me for a mere four to six seconds. And, I suppose, I hated my agency for having placed me in that position. Unfortunately for me, the employees assistance program was not established until two years after my shooting. I will never be able to adequately express my gratitude to headquarters and the employees assistance program for making that seminar available to me . . . and for making me attend!

If I had the opportunity to share what I've learned with my fellow law enforcement officers, here's what I'd tell them:

1. We are vulnerable, and we can have our control taken from us. IT REALLY CAN HAPPEN TO YOU! We must do all that we can to physically, mentally, and emotionally prepare ourselves for the trauma of a critical incident.

2. It is normal to have a reaction to a critical incident, even if we are on the periphery and not directly involved. That reaction may be mild, moderate, or severe. Any type of reaction is normal considering this abnormal event.

3. Take advantage of a peer support group or additional professional counseling. Although we want to stand tough and do it alone, we cannot be an island. Don't wait nine and a half years to accept help that now will be made available to you shortly after your incident. Take advantage of whatever help is offered you and realize that you are not the first to suffer this kind of tragedy, and you don't have to suffer it alone.

4. For those of you who must have contact with this individual, be gentle. Even the most innocent remark can be devastating in this individual's state of emotional hypersensitivity. We don't consider ourselves "head cases," and we don't consider ourselves heroes. We are just ordinary people who have been through extraordinary experiences . . . and we are still ordinary people.

A NEEDLESS DEATH ON A BEAUTIFUL DAY

Sometimes it seems that tragedy begets tragedy. Too often, a family that has suffered one tremendous blow receives another just a year or two later. Stories like these make even the casual listener shiver with horror. "How can so many terrible things happen to one family?" we ask, trying to imagine how we would survive if so many tragedies befell us, and not knowing the answer.

What happened to Officer Dan Gleason of the Philadelphia Police Department and his family is one of those terrible stories—a story of pain, and devastation, and courage you never wanted to be forced to have.

Pam Gleason found that courage somewhere, somehow, after her husband was killed. "Dan was my hero. I idolized him. But he never thought he was anything special."

Those were Pam's closing comments to me when I interviewed her by telephone on August 3, 1989. A trustee in the COPS (Concerns of Police Survivors) group, Pam had been recommended as someone I needed to talk to for this book. She gave me two hours of her time, speaking from a friend's borrowed telephone in a vacation trailer in Cape May Court House, New Jersey.

In those two hours, Pam told me about Dan's line-of-duty death three years before, and she told me of her own survival. Dan and Pam had six children; when Dan was killed, their youngest was three months old. Since his death, Pam was managing to carry on, attempting to be both mother and father to their children.

It was tough, she said. It was lonely. There were tears in her voice at the end of the interview. I was impressed by her honesty and her vulnerability, her strength and her generosity of spirit. As a founder of the Southeast Delaware Valley chapter of COPS, Pam was doing a lot for other survivors. I thanked Pam, asked her to send me some news clippings about Dan when she got home from vacation, and filed my notes away for the time being.

Not two weeks later, just as I was sitting down to write Pam and Dan's story for this book, I got a phone call from Betty Miller, another police widow active in COPS.

"I thought somebody ought to tell you," she said. "You interviewed Pam Gleason, didn't you?" I confirmed that I had.

Betty was crying. "I don't know how to say this, but Pam is gone. She's dead."

My mind raced backwards to my telephone interview with Pam nine days before. No, it was impossible, Pam couldn't be dead, not with those six children depending on her!

But it was true. Pamela Gleason died on August 13, 1989. A passenger in a car driven by a drunk driver, she was killed instantly when the car ran into a tree.

I looked back over my interview notes, and there were the children's names, with their ages at the time of their father's line-of-duty death just three years ago:

Danny 15
Irene 14
Barry 8

Mandy 3
Judy 2
Craig 3 months

Now they were not just fatherless children. They were orphans.

Danny would be 18 now. Since his father's death, he had a sense of responsibility for the family. Pam had told me that he was worried about heading for college in the fall. "Will anything get done around here without me?" he'd ask his mother.

I wonder if Danny will make it to college this year, with his mother gone.

I wonder if little Craig will remember either of his parents.

I wonder why both parents had to be ripped away from the children they loved so much.

Looking for answers, I went back to the newspaper clippings, the fading pages that tell the story of what happened to their father. There are no answers to my "Why's" there—only the recounting of what Pam Gleason called "a needless death on such a beautiful day."

The first of the two young parents died on June 5, 1986.

In North Philadelphia on that sunny morning, a man named Nathan Long said that Allah was speaking to him. "I am the instrument of Allah," Long said.

Nathan Long had a criminal record. He had been arrested on charges of riot, assault and battery, resisting arrest, and obstruction of justice after assaulting a police officer. He was found guilty of obstruction of justice and received a suspended sentence. Two warrants were out for his arrest: He had shot and wounded a neighbor, and he was a suspect in a burglary case.

When Dan and his partner, rookie Laurine Venable, answered the disturbance call on West Sedgely Avenue that bright morning, they didn't know who Nathan Long was. They didn't know they were about to confront a violent man who always carried a gun, a man whose apartment was full of gun publications, a man who received murderous marching orders from his God.

Long was enraged about the growing prostitution activity in his neighborhood. That morning, he encountered a prostitute sitting in a car with a customer. Long accused the man of wearing a shirt stolen from Long's house. Then he picked up a baseball bat and began to smash the windows of the car. Several other people got involved in the brawl.

When Officers Gleason and Venable arrived, Dan went to talk to Nathan Long, around the corner from the other people involved in the incident. Laurine Venable stopped to talk with them. A low-key, gentle man, Dan Gleason was good at defusing angry situations. He had calmed arguments like these many times before. But this time, he didn't get a chance.

In court, Nathan Long testified that the officer came up to him and very politely asked, "Good morning, what can I do for you today?"

Nathan Long's answer was six bullets fired from a semiautomatic weapon.

Three bullets hit Dan Gleason in the head. Two more glanced off the bullet-resistant vest he was wearing, one of them piercing the pictures of Dan's kids in his breast pocket. Another bullet struck Dan in the right arm.

Even if he'd had time to return fire, Dan probably

wouldn't have, Pam told me, because there was an eight-year-old boy near the shooting scene. "Dan would never have fired his gun with a child that close by."

Officer Venable was still talking to Nathan Long's neighbors when she heard the shots ring out. Courageously, she ran at once toward the gunfire. Assuming a firing position, she shot at the suspect. When she ran out of bullets, she took Dan's revolver and fired again, hitting Long twice in the arm. Her shots did not stop him immediately. He got into his car and drove away, but his wounds forced him to drive to a hospital, where police arrested him.

"I think she's a hero," Pam Gleason said of Officer Venable, who was devastated by her partner's death. "When she came to our home the day before the funeral, all of Dan's brothers and sisters—our whole family—stood up and applauded her."

But Laurine Venable's courageous actions could not save Dan Gleason. He was pronounced dead at 10:22 a.m. at Temple University Hospital.

That started Pam Gleason's long nightmare.

The police officers who came to notify her of Dan's death did their best to help her. "The captain took the baby out of my arms. They went and got my kids out of school. They took me to the hospital. I had to really push to be allowed to see Dan. I could only a see a small portion of his face.

"He had told me, 'If I go, don't bury anything. Give it all away.' But all I could do was donate his eyes and his skin."

There was the funeral—a five-mile-long motorcade. There were the immediate demands of six children—two of them in diapers!—to be met. "All my kids got real sick that summer," Pam remembered. "I think it was a combination of physical and psychological things. I'd get to bed at 2 a.m. and get up at 4 a.m. That was the only time the baby would let me sleep."

Then there was Nathan Long's trial dragging on for weeks. Pam sat in the courtroom day after day. "There was one person who wasn't represented in that courtroom, and it was Dan," she said. "I had to be there for him. People had to see that it was more than a badge that died that day."

Victims in the courtroom are often warned by the prosecuting attorney not to show any overt emotion. A mistrial can be declared if a weeping victim or survivor can be proved to have influenced the jurors. In fact, when an aunt hugged eight-year-old Barry Gleason, who had gotten upset in the courtroom, the judge ordered them both removed.

Determined to stay in the courtroom for Dan's sake, Pam sat through dramatic testimony about her husband's killing and his injuries, never breaking down.

It came out in court that Nathan Long had planned for 10 years to kill a policeman. "I thought that constituted premeditated murder, but the jury didn't see it that way," Pam said. Nathan Long was found guilty of murder and received a life sentence. After 12 years, he can petition the Governor of Pennsylvania to change his sentence to a specific number of years instead of life. If this ever happens, he will become eligible for parole.

"We may have a lifetime of fighting ahead of us to keep this from happening," Pam said.

Sadly, Pam did not have a lifetime. She had just another nine days to live.

Pam told me about the lowest moment she experienced after Dan's death. It was about a year later. "I was at the kitchen sink, up to my elbows in pots and pans. Three of the kids were hanging on me, and the other three were fighting and screaming in the next room. I was exhausted and miserable, and I said to Dan, 'How in hell can you be happy in heaven when I'm so damn miserable down here?'"

It was a turning point for Pam, who soon realized that maybe Dan wasn't happy in heaven: "Maybe he couldn't be until I got it together."

The Gleasons had the kind of marriage many people only dream about. "If you knew Pam, you knew Dan, and vice versa," Pam recalled. "We didn't have any money. He was just a cop and we had all these kids. So we did everything ourselves and we did everything together. He'd change diapers and wash dishes, I'd change the oil in the car. All he ever wanted to do was be with his family."

Pam's love for Dan was still obvious three years after his death. "He was so handsome," she told me, "six feet tall, 165 pounds—slim, though he could eat like a horse—curly brown hair, blue eyes with those disgustingly long eyelashes. All my sons have inherited them."

In spite of her tremendous loss, Pam went forward, founding a COPS chapter in her region, reaching out to other survivors, and taking care of her and Dan's six children. Her faith helped her. But, she told me, "I'm still having a few arguments with God about this whole thing."

Pam wanted very much to see the National Law Enforcement Officers Memorial completed. "I'm so thrilled with this monument, and not so much for those who died, but for anyone that is, has, or ever will wear a badge. They do a very unpleasant job and get spit on in return. It's about time police were given the same honor and dignity as military veterans. They deserve it, and it's part of the healing process."

Certainly Dan Gleason deserved that permanent tribute. So did Pam. And so do their children.

As I write this, Pam Gleason's funeral is taking place in Philadelphia, at the same church where Dan's funeral was held a little over three years ago. "I can't help feeling there's half of me buried in that ground with Dan," she told me.

Today she will join him.

AFTERWORD

For Dan Gleason and for Donna Miller . . . for Phil Lamonaco and for Ariel Rios . . . for John Davis and for Mike Raburn, and for all the officers who have willingly given up their lives in service to the community, the National Law Enforcement Officers Memorial will stand as a tribute to their courage and their sacrifice.

For their spouses and their children, their parents and their brothers and sisters, the Memorial will be a place of healing. It will keep precious memories alive, and say, "Your suffering and your loss have not gone unnoticed."

For the officers still serving today and for all those who will serve in the future, the Memorial is a symbol of this nation's appreciation for their dedicated service, a symbol of America's commitment to the principles of law and order they live and die for.

What will this Memorial, so meaningful to so many, look like?

It will occupy a city block in the heart of our nation's capital, a place called, appropriately, Judiciary Square, just blocks from the Capitol and the Supreme Court, just minutes from the Washington Monument, the Jefferson and Lincoln Memorials, the Vietnam Veterans Memorial, and The White House.

A row of stately trees will form an oval enclosure, creating a serene, grove-like atmosphere for remembrance. Low granite walls, polished to a high sheen, will be engraved with the names of officers lost in the line of duty. Benches near the walls will allow visitors to pause and reflect in comfort.

Life-like statues of law enforcement officers will grace the Memorial plaza. And, every evening, the Memorial Fund wants to shine a crystal-blue laser beam high into the night sky, representing the "thin blue line" of police protection that stands between ordinary citizens and criminals.

It will be a dignified, beautiful place—a fitting tribute to the thousands of law enforcement officers who have given up their lives to protect our American way of life.

But it can only be built with the financial support of *all* the American people. Please do your part. Send your tax-deductible contribution to:

The National Law Enforcement Officers
Memorial Fund
1360 Beverly Road, Suite 305
McLean, Virginia 22101

The names and home towns of donors will be inscribed in a special Roll of Honor to be kept with the Memorial's Archives.

Please, let the families of fallen law enforcement heroes know that you care. Help build the long-overdue National Law Enforcement Officers Memorial. Thank you.